James Carmichael

Organic Union of Canadian Churches

With a Comparison of Authorized Standards

James Carmichael

Organic Union of Canadian Churches
With a Comparison of Authorized Standards

ISBN/EAN: 9783337162405

Printed in Europe, USA, Canada, Australia, Japan

Cover: Foto ©ninafisch / pixelio.de

More available books at **www.hansebooks.com**

ORGANIC UNION

OF CANADIAN CHURCHES:

WITH A

COMPARISON OF AUTHORISED STANDARDS.

BY THE

VERY REV. JAMES CARMICHAEL, M.A., D.C.L.

DEAN OF MONTREAL.

MONTREAL:

DAWSON BROTHERS, PUBLISHERS.

1887.

In the spirit of the resolution passed unanimously by the last Provincial Synod of the Church of England in Canada on the subject of Christian Union, this work is written and compiled with the hope that it may prove of some slight service to those who are anxious " to follow after the things which make for peace."

St. George's Rectory,
Montreal, April, 1887.

TABLE OF CONTENTS.

CHURCH UNITY.

The question of Church Unity is one that has been forcing itself, in some shape or another, on the minds of Christian people for many years past; and, as time advances, the feeling in its favour grows stronger. Out of this feeling have arisen two schemes: one for the union of Christendom, the other for the union of Protestant Churches. The former is not without able and earnest advocates in the Church of England, in representatives of the Old Catholic movement, and has had its advocates in the Church of Rome, men who hold, or have held, that our divisions are by no means irreconcilable, and that, if we only sought for peace, instead of victory, peace would win the victory in time. The advocates of the latter scheme assert that union with Rome, until Rome reforms herself, is an impossibility, that union with the Greek and Eastern Churches is at present an improbability, but that corporato union between the leading Protestant Colonial Churches is not alone possible, but practicable, if only the guiding minds of the great Protestant systems in any one colony met together in a Christian spirit to take the whole subject into earnest consideration, and inaugurate the movement.

ARGUMENTS IN FAVOUR OF PROTESTANT UNION.

The advocates for Protestant union argue in this fashion.

(1.) The will and purpose of our Lord is, that His church should " be one ;" (Matt. xvi. 18 ; John xvii. 21-22) and hence it is the duty of His children who, though divided, are not hopelessly so, to strive, as far as possible, to bring about union, even in a limited degree ; as an example and prophecy of a wider unity.

(2.) That two-thirds of the human race are still strangers to any form of Christianity, that the divisions of Christians raise up a barrier in the heathen mind against the doctrines of Christianity, and that, consequently, those least divided should strive and come together to diminish the evils caused by division.

(3.) That the spirituality of Christian thought—its higher and purer life,—is dwarfed and weakened, and in some cases, positively destroyed by our unhappy divisions ; as evidenced by what may be seen in any small Canadian village, where three or four religious systems minister to twelve hundred people, and where " the Cause," rather than " the Christ," becomes too often the motive power of missionary exertion.

(4.) That the points of religious agreement on fundamental doctrines, are far more numerous than the points of difference; that the things which naturally unite us are greater in number, and importance than the things which divide us.

(5.) That, if unity be God's will and plan, and we rest calmly contented with division, once the Spirit of God breathing on the public mind awakes it to its responsibilities, then we are guilty of a positive sin if we set our faces against the " things which make for peace."

(6.) That, if unity be God's will, and our disunion is out of touch with that will, we should always bear in mind that " with God nothing is impossible," —in other words, that union amongst the divided brethren of the Reformation is not an impossibility.

(7.) That we are not without precedents of happy success in other fields which should lead us on hopefully to inaugurate a movement in the interests of unity. Such a movement, like the Temperance movement, might take eighty or ninety years to obtain legislation; or, like emancipation from slavery, it might take only fifteen years ; but it would be in the hands of that God with whom " one day is as a " thousand years and a thousand years as one day," and with that God, nothing is impossible.

(8.) The advocates of Protestant union, whilst recognizing more and more the points of contact between all Protestant Churches, in no way shut their eyes to the points of difference. But their trust is in God and time, and a free and equal interchange of brotherly opinion, through properly constituted deliberative committees meeting together in a Christian spirit, meeting for work, not for sentimentality and poetic laudations of each others' charms. They hold that the sentimentality of the question has had its day, and that it has now taken its place within the field of practical religious politics.

CANADA, AS A FIELD TO TEST THE MOVEMENT IN.

The advocates for Protestant union also feel that Canada furnishes an admirable field to test the movement in.

(1.) Because the desire for unity has already found public and legal expression in Canada, two of the great Protestant Churches having appointed representatives to talk over the general question, namely : the Church of England and the Methodist Church. The Presbyterian and other churches would, no doubt, have appointed representatives, if the proposition (emanating from the Church of England) had reached their respective synods and assemblies in time to enable them to do so.

(2.) Because, in Canada, the old vexed question of Church and State is swept out of the road, not one solitary vestige of the controversy being left behind. As churches possessed of the power of making our own laws, we are free, free as air ; any two churches, or five, or for the matter of that all, having power to come together and make any kind of organic union they desire.

(3.) Because, in Canada, the principle of union has been triumphantly tested by both the Presbyterian and Methodist Churches within the field of their respective divisions.

(4.) Because, in Canada, the distinctive forms of government, in all the churches, work very much on the same lines through clergy and laity, in systems of Vestries, Presbyteries, Synods, Assemblies, Conferences, Dioceses, Circuits, etc.,—different names that mean very much the same thing, as far as practical government is concerned.

(5.) Because, through the freedom of church life in Canada, each great Protestant Church has unconsciously been learning from sister churches, and thus drawing closer together in action, although dividing lines may to the eye appear as strong as ever.

Having thus stated the broad arguments in favour of Protestant union, and those in favour of inaugurating the movement in Canada, I would now outline the historical aspect of the Church in its undivided, and divided aspects.

HISTORICAL OUTLINE OF "THE CHURCH" AT UNITY WITH HERSELF.

If we go back to the spirit and letter of the Acts of the Apostles and Epistles, it is perfectly plain on

the face of these documents, that the Church of God
was one great undivided church, and that there is
nothing in the New Testament analagous to the de-
nominational system. We read of churches in different
countries, but they are branches of the parent church
in Jerusalem; so much so that Jerusalem decided the
great question of Christian circumcision for the
churches of Antioch, Syria and Cilicia. (Acts xv. 19.)
Then the teaching of St. Paul clearly implies the
oneness of the Church, pre-eminently in Col. i. 18-24-
25, where he compares the whole Church of God,
the world over, to the human body, of which he says,
" Christ is the head." Of which Church, " he (St.
Paul) was made a minister," in which there should be
no "schism," or split, or separation or division, and
in which Christ had set apostles, and prophets, and
teachers, and miracle workers, to exercise their gifts
in unison ; just as the nerves and sinews and muscles
work together in unity—one body. In short, in reading the Acts of the Apostles and Epistles, we are
brought into an atmosphere of organic unity.
Of course, we find different aspects of doctrine, different usages, habits and customs, party spirit and party
disputes, but all these things are included within the
bounds of the one ever growing Church, marching
onward in giant strength, and sweeping all before it,
under the rule of the Apostles and the guidance of
the Holy Spirit of God.

PATRISTIC AGE.

In the age of the early Christian fathers, this great
church idea becomes more and more apparent. Rent

and torn as we are, it is hard to realize what these men felt as they saw this new born force—the Church—literally dragging them along to the most magnificent victories for the Lord Jesus. "The Church" to them was a divine thing, instituted by Christ, washing itself daily in the blood of martyrs, and starting on a mission that was never to cease till the whole world laid its trophies at the feet of the Lord Jesus—"Head of the Church triumphant." And if, in their burning love for the dear Lord and His offspring, they, hot-blooded Easterns, at times used language descriptive of this Church that we, cold-blooded Westerns, could never dream of using, what after all is such luxuriance of language, such richness of metaphor, but love, akin to that which led the holy Mary to break the alabaster box upon our Saviour's feet, " till the whole house was " filled with the odour of the ointment." It was love, loyalty, and devotion to Jesus. Would to God we had it, and we would not be the stranded wrecks we are.

TESTIMONY OF THE FATHERS TO THE ONENESS OF THE CHURCH.

The testimony of these Fathers to the oneness of the Church is undeviating. *Clement*, whose epistle to the Corinthians is saturated with Christly teaching, speaks of the visible organized church as "one Body working harmoniously for the preservation of the whole." (1 Ep. xxvii., xxviii.) *Ignatius* states that the officers of the Church were settled everywhere to the bounds of the earth by the will of the Lord Jesus. (Epis Eph. iii.) He writes of "the whole Church" (cap. v.), of "God breathing immortality into His Church" (cap. xvii.), of "the harmony of God in His Church" (cap. xv.), of "the Church of God's Mercy" and "the Church of God's Love" (Epis Rom.), of "the Church of God the Father" (Intro. Epis Phil.), of "the body of Christ His Church" (Epis Smyr. 1), of the "Catholic or Universal Church" (viii.), and of "the Church which has received grace through the greatness of God Most High." Whatever controversy there may be as to the recensions of the Ignatian Epistles, one thing is certain, that none of them teach denominationalism, or touch on any thought approaching it, except where they warn the local churches against divisions, and controversies that can only breed confusion.

In the writings of *Irenæus* directed against heresies, the great thought underlying the whole of these apologies, is the oneness of the Church instituted by Christ; that the truth is to be found nowhere else but in the one Catholic Church; that she is the sole depository of apostolic doctrine; and that heresies are of recent formation and cannot trace their origin up to the Apostles. This is the keynote of his whole work —an appeal to the oneness and universality of the Church of Jesus.

EARLIEST BREACHES OF UNITY.

This oneness, however, was not without breaches being made in it at a comparatively early period, but in every case, the great Church passed on "conquering and to conquer," and in due time received back into her

bosom the representatives of those who in angry
moments caused the early schisms. The breach of
Montanism was closed in the fourth century as if it
had never been made, although the principle asserted
by it, that the Church was a spiritual rather than a
secular power remains, thank God, within the scattered
fold to-day. The breach of Novatianism taught the
lesson of loyalty to Christ and of devotion to death
for the baptism of the Lord, but the sect died out in
the fourth century, largely under the influence of the
eighth canon of the Council of Nice, which provided
for the re-admission of the Novatian clergy to the
Catholic Church. The breach of Donatism taught its
lesson of "the higher life," but at the close of the
fifth century the vast bulk of the Donatists were
re-absorbed into the Church, and, at the beginning of
the seventh, the schism was wholly healed. The
breach of Arianism kept open until the middle of the
sixth century, but the overwhelming power of the
One Church won the victory—as a united Church will
always win—and gradually "the very name 'Arian'
ceased to represent a definite form of Christian doctrine within the Church, or a definite party outside
of it." The great bosom of the Great Mother lay
bare for wandering and wearied children to lay their
heads on; generation after generation sought the resting place, and at last the moment came, when Arianism,
the deadliest foe of the Catholic Church, existed as a
distinctive sect no longer. There were anxious moments in the history of some of these schisms, when
the life of the mother seemed imperilled (pre-eminently
during the Arian controversy) but some way the tide

turned at the right moment, and the great Church found thronging round her feet her alien or her straying children. A wondrous, and ever opening fulfilment of the divine promise, monopolized by Rome, twisted and contorted again and again through the long ages, but true—true to the very letter,—" Lo I am with you always, even to the end of the world."

THE RUPTURE BETWEEN THE EAST AND WEST.

From this period onward to the great rupture between its eastern and western branches, the Church maintained its oneness. But, from the sixth to the eleventh century, a growing estrangement took place between the Western branch, as represented by the Bishop of Rome, and the Eastern branch, represented by the Patriarch of Constantinople. Arguments and controversies arose on deep doctrinal matters ; such as the person of the Holy Ghost; and on other subjects, such as image worship, the seventh day Sabbath, the marriage of the clergy, lenten discipline, and confirmation. But, underlying all such controversies, was the thirst of Rome for universal power and supreme spiritual rule over the whole Church ; leading to the excommunication by Rome of Photius, Patriarch of Constantinople, who, in quick reply, excommunicated Nicholas, Bishop of Rome. Then came Hildebrand, with his claim to the universal oversight of the whole Church, and his demand of submission to the chair of St. Peter, and then the final break in the year 1054, when the Roman legates excommunicated the Greek patriarch in his own Church of St. Sophia in Constantinople, and, flinging down the anathema of Rome upon the great altar, shook off the dust of the West against the East, and, through lust of power rather than through difference of opinion, created a breach that has lasted to the present hour, spite of the famous attempt at reconciliation made at a council held in Florence in 1438.

FROM THE GREAT RUPTURE TO THE PROTESTANT REFORMATION.

From the great rupture between East and West, down to the Reformation, is a long stretch of 463 years; during which time the great Crusades shook the world, Tartar and Turk swept all before them, England ate out her vitals through the wars of the Roses, America was discovered, and the national boundaries of the map of the world were changed again and again. But there was one giant influence that grew and prospered, in spiritual power, in iron grasp of authority, in additions and accretions of doctrine, —an influence that extended itself in France, in Germany, in England, all over the West—the influence of the Church of Rome. Its departure from the apostolic and primitive faith of the church had been as great as it was saddening. It had prohibited the Bible in native tongues, established the doctrines of transubstantiation and the celibacy of the clergy, opened out the question of the Immaculate Conception of the Blessed Virgin, published the renowned Bull that all things were under papal jurisdiction, invented and taught the value of Indulgences, established as an engine of deadly power the Inquisition, and burnt Huss and Jerome of Prague, at the stake. There were thousands of good and holy men and saintly women within the pale of Rome and of all Western churches, but the influence, the example, and the power of Rome was as leaven everywhere; and, as that influence extended, primitive faith and practical morality declined with it. The popes were recognized as God's vice-gerents on earth by the various national churches of the West; and Alexander the Sixth, the infamous Rodrigo Borgia, a wretch whose life makes one positively ashamed of human nature, was one of God's vice-gerents. With such possible leaders, and the influence proceeding from them throughout all churches, little wonder that the clergy, as a rule, were immoral, dishonest, and ignorant; and less wonder that the people who depended on them for education were degraded to the lowest depths of degradation. Pope Adrian VI. openly declared, in the Diet of Nuremburg in 1522, that " everything in the church had been perverted and that a disease had spread from the head to the members, from the popes to the rest of the rulers of the church." In short, the church throughout the West, ordained by God to purify the West, had, through the subtle influence and example of Rome, become the prime source of its corruption; and just as Abel's blood called to God for vengeance, so the voices of all that were pure in the various churches called out for deliverance from the church itself distorted and defiled; and then came the glorious doctrinal Reformation of the sixteenth century, with Luther and Melancthon,

Zwingle and Calvin, Martyr and Bucer, Cranmer, Latimer and Ridley, to guide it under God to its consummation.

THE PROTESTANT REFORMATION IN ENGLAND.

The Reformation in England was reflective rather than original. It reflected Germany and the continental divines. It produced magnificent heroes, but no giant minds like Luther or Calvin. Perhaps the greatest influence for waking up England against the influence and power of Rome and of determination to resist it, came from Rome itself, in the person of Cardinal Pole, who, letting loose the horrors of persecution during the reign of Mary, gave the English people a detestation of popery that has shown itself stronger in England for the last three centuries than in any other nation of the west, for, whilst half Germany has gone back to Rome, England, to-day, is the most intensely Protestant nation on the face of the earth. The Church of England came forth finally from the crucible of Reformation in the days of Charles I., a reformed, rather than a re-organized church. It was, as far as original government was concerned, the same Church that had been established in Britain long previous to the landing of Augustine on the shores of Kent, and that had been represented at the council of Arles, A.D. 303, and summoned to the synods of Sardica (347) and Rimini (360). However the mists of time and lack of records may have clouded evidence for the unbroken historic continuity of the old British church, the continuity of orders, from Augustine through the See of Canterbury, had never been injuriously interrupted. The English Church, previous to, and after the Reformation, was just as much the same church, as Naaman was Naaman, after he had washed away his leprosy in the river Jordan. In a word, the the Church reformed, but did not re-organize ; the succession to the archbishopric of Canterbury being maintained through all the throes of Reformation, as follows :

Archbishop Wareham, in direct line from
  Augustine.................................. 1503
Archbishop Cranmer.................. 1533
Cardinal Pole 1556
Archbishop Parker...................... 1559
Archbishop Grendall.................... 1576

The evidence for the due consecration of Archbishop Parker is found in the following facts : (1) Documentary evidence of the consecration of Bishops Scory, Coverdale and Hodgkins, and circumstantial evidence as to the consecration of Bishop Barlow, arising from the fact, that he was cited under Royal warrant to consecrate ; (2) The registers of Canterbury ; (3) The warrant of consecration under the Great Seal ; (4) The original instrument of consecration in the library of Corpus Christi College, Cambridge ; (5) Testimony of the Earl of Nottingham who was present at Parker's consecration. (See in connection with general subject of consecration, Col. of Nicea, can. iv., Col. Chalcedon Act, 16 ; 3rd Col. of Carthage, can. xxxix.)

The rule of reformation which the Church of England followed was that of throwing off everything it believed Rome had added to the Christian Faith; but of retaining even what was characteristic of Rome, provided it agreed with Scripture and the usage of the primitive church. Thus it retained as matters of deepest importance the three orders of the ministry, the rite of confirmation, and a liturgical service based on the Christian year, clerical dress and other minor matters, none of which it held were the actual fruits of the papacy. But, as a reformed church, it rejected :—the supremacy of the pope, worship of images, invocation of saints, the Latin tongue in service, the sacramental character of confirmation, penance, holy orders, matrimony and extreme unction; restored the cup to the laity, rejected the doctrines that surrounded the Mass, as "blasphemous fables and dangerous deceits," permitted the marriage of the clergy, declared that every National Church had a right to govern itself, and that the Bishop of Rome had no jurisdiction in the realm of England. In short, possessed of an unbroken historic succession, the Church of England rose wholly independent of, and antagonistic to, Rome, and proceeded to propagate her cleansed and purified organic life as a true branch of the primitive and apostolic Church of the Lord Jesus.

THE PROTESTANT REFORMATION IN IRELAND.

The organized Irish Church founded by St. Patrick in A.D. 432 was identical in doctrine with the church in Britain and Gaul and with all the Western churches. The government consisted of an abbot or head of

the monastic rule of each tribe; and bishops, priests
and deacons, the bishops being in some respects subject to the abbot, who generally, though not necessarily, was a presbyter, although the ordaining and
confirming powers of the bishops were fully recognized and never encroached upon. After the death
of St. Patrick, the Irish Church, through Columban,
Aiden, Cuthbert, Cædmon and others, flung itself into
the missionary work of the church with such success
" that it seemed at one time as if Celtic Christianity
and not Latin was to mould the destinies of the
churches of the West." Then came the struggle with
the Danes, the establishment of the Danish Church
with orders from Canterbury, the double line of holy
orders through Armagh and Canterbury; then the
transfer in 1164, by Pope Adrian the Fourth, of
Ireland to England, in order that Henry II. might
"subdue it and enlarge the bounds of the Church,"
and then the long resisted yet final bringing of the
Church in Ireland under the influence and doctrine of
the Church of Rome.

The history of the Reformation in Ireland is the
history of a mistake. The problem should have been
how to bring under the reforming influence, a quick-
witted people ("not scholars," writes Archbishop
Browne, " yet crafty to cozen,") who were foreigners
to England, speaking a language totally different from
the English language, and trained under the influence
of Rome to worship God, according to the ritual of
the Latin Mass. The obvious remedy for this was
authorized Irish translations of the Bible and liturgy
placed in the hands of priests and people coupled with

an educational system carried on in the Irish tongue. But, from the beginning, the work was bungled. In 1536, an Act was proclaimed for encouraging "the English order, habit, and language ; which required that spiritual promotion should be given 'only to such as could speak English, unless after four proclamations in the nearest market, such could not be had.' The same Act further enjoined that parochial English schools should be established in the country, and that all clergymen should learn and teach English, and preach the Word of God in English," (Irish statutes, Henry VIII., c. viii.) An English form of prayer called the "Form of Beads " was also set forth, which was about as useful as an English Prayer Book would be to the latest discovered tribe in Central Africa. In 1551, instructions came to " propagate the worship of God in the English tongue; the service to be translated into Irish in those places which need it," this latter clause, however, was not carried out. On the accession of Elizabeth, the English service was again used, and the Act of uniformity passed, containing the singularly injudicious clause that, in places where the English tongue could not be used, worship might be conducted in the Latin tongue, " for that also the same may not be in their native language," on account of printing difficulties, ignorance of people, etc. Then followed the patriotic efforts of Walshe and Kearney, Donellan and Bedell, resulting in an Irish catechism in 1571, the translation of the New Testament, which was not published, however, till 1603, the translation of the Common Prayer published in 1608, and the translation of the

B

Old Testament published in 1685—admirable works
of devotion and learning, but resulting in little use to
the people, as no authoritative effort was made by the
crown to disseminate the translations amongst the
people. Thus the use of the Latin tongue practically
became a necessity of worship amongst the Celtic
Irish,—a fact worth untold riches to the Church of
Rome, when in 1615, it sent to Ireland, a titular
episcopate, which assumed, by virtue of papal grants,
the titles and jurisdiction of the Irish prelates, who
as direct successors of St. Patrick, had embraced the
doctrines of the Reformation.

The Reformation in Ireland resulted in three distinct
aspects of Church life : (1) The Reformed Church of
Ireland carrying out its life in double succession
from Armagh and Canterbury. (2) The dissentient
mission of the Church of Rome governed by titular
bishops (the nucleus of the present Romish Church in
Ireland), a government styled by the legal Bishop of
Derry in 1622, as " a jurisdiction usurped by authority
from Rome, to the great dishonor of God, hinderance
of religion, and shame of the government." (3) Congregations of Protestant non-conformists widely extended through various parts of Ulster.

THE PROTESTANT REFORMATION IN SCOTLAND.

The church in Scotland was a branch of the one unbroken church that had come down from primitive
times. Originally, it received the faith from Ireland
through St. Columban, and adopted the Irish form of
government—bishops, priests and deacons—with the

Presbyter Abbot of Iona, the successor of St. Columban, as Primate of the church. This primacy, in the ninth century, seems to have been transferred to the Abbot of Dunkeld, and afterwards merged wholly in the Bishopric of St. Andrews; and from that period onward to the Reformation, the government of the church was wholly episcopal.

The influence of Rome in Scotland was just as powerful as in England, or anywhere else; and the Scottish bishops, previous to the period of the Reformation, had come to be regarded as the degraded representatives of a foreign tyranny. Hence when Knox brought his giant besom to sweep out the defiled temple, he swept the bishops out before him like chaff on a threshing floor and modelled the government of the Reformed church after the fashion of that established by Calvin in Geneva. This, however, before long, gave way to a scheme whereby the old episcopal sees were filled with new born Protestant bishops consecrated by a chapter of learned ministers, a move that brought about the agitation headed by Andrew Melville, which resulted in the establishment of the Presbyterian system of government. Then came the re-establishment of Episcopacy in the reign of King James, gaining its succession from Canterbury, then the restoration of Presbytery under the Covenanters, then, at the restoration of the Monarchy, the re-establishment of Episcopacy, and finally, in the reign of William and Mary, the Presbyterian Church of Scotland was definitely established, the Westminster Confession ratified, the General Assembly recognized as a legislative body, and from that day to this, Presbyterianism has run its course as an independent, powerful and singularly devoted portion of the once united church.

THE REFORMATION AND THE INDEPENDENTS.

The Churches of England and Scotland were reformed legally through the action of the state, and from this use of the state in reforming, there arose in England a school of religious thought which repudiated the interference of the state altogether. "The church," it said, "is of Christ, not of the State, it was founded by the Apostles of the living God, and its mission is to convert and lead the state, rather than be led by it." The followers of this school of religious thought were called Independents. The first Independent Church was established in England in 1616, and in 1620, the first colony of Independents landed on the shores of North America, and proceeded to lay the foundation of the New England States,—the fore-runners of the great Puritan and Independent immigration, which led to the ultimate formation of the American system of Congregationalism. The success of Independency in America, exercised a strong influence in favour of both the organization and its teaching in England, and, as a result, the iron hand of Archbishop Laud endeavored to repress it. With the fall of Laud, came the onward progress of Independency—onward through its battlings with Presbyterianism—onward till it became the great semi-religious political power of the commonwealth under Cromwell. Then, with the restoration of the Monarchy, came its downfall

as a political power and its religious life had a limited
field of liberty until, under the Hanoverian dynasty,
it gained a freer life, and, from that time onward to
the present, it has steadily obtained in England equal
liberty of worship and action with all other Protestant churches outside of the Establishment. In
America, Congregationalism is a great religious force,
numbering its churches by thousands, and possessed
of seven Theological Institntions.

METHODISM.

The history of Methodism may be fairly divided
into two sections. (1) Its history inside the Church
of England. (2) Its history outside the Church of
England.

Its history inside the church, may be described as
that of an honest Christian effort on the part of
godly men, most of them clergymen of the Church
of England, to form religious societies for the purpose
of arousing men to a sense of sin and the need of salvation, and for deepening the spiritual lives of those
who professed to be followers of the Lord Jesus.
These societies were divided into classes, the leaders
being laymen, acting under Wesley and other priests
of the Church of England ; and one great work of the
leader was that of seeing that the members were
regular attendants at the services of the Church of
England, and at its holy table. As time advanced,
and property accumulated, Wesley saw the need of
forming some kind of a legislative body to take the
oversight of these societies, and the properties con-

nected with them. Hence he formed what he called "The Legal Conference," consisting of one hundred itinerant lay preachers, named by himself; and he vested in these lay preachers the general oversight and direction of the missionary operations, and the management of all the societies; keeping however, for himself, summary and supreme jurisdiction as head and visitor of the whole organization. Up to this time, Wesley would not allow the organization to call itself a church. In all deeds and public documents, and in all Wesley's letters, it is called "A Society," the Society of the people called Methodists, "the Methodist Society," etc. All its members, who were not professed dissenters, were regarded as belonging naturally to the Church of England; for it must be borne in mind, that it was by no means necessary, at this stage of Methodist history, that a man should leave his own church to become a Methodist. There were Methodists who were Baptists, Methodists who were Presbyterians, and, largely, Methodists who belonged to the Church of England— one great secret of the early success of the organization.

The history of Methodism, outside of the Church of England, practically dates from the time that Wesley ordained Coke, as Superintendent for work in the American colonies; and some of the English lay preachers to act as ministers in Scotland and England. From that time forth, the idea of a distinct and separate ministry grew up in the societies, until at last, in 1834, a theological institution was established, and in 1836, the practice of ordination by the imposition of hands was adopted, and Methodism floated out from the Mother Church, a distinct and separate church body, carrying with it a large share of the theology of the Church of England, and a zeal and devotion in the service of Christ worthy of the days of the Apostles.

Having thus given an outline history of the four great systems of ecclesiastical government, which in England and her colonies, represent the united result of the English Reformation, we may now ask, which of these systems might naturally come together in consultation, to speak over differences, and to initiate, if possible, a movement through their respective governing bodies, for organic union, as a step towards a larger union ?   In reply, we would humbly submit, that the systems that ought naturally to come together are :—

  (1) THE EPISCOPAL SYSTEM.
  (2) THE PRESBYTERIAN SYSTEM.
  (3) THE METHODIST SYSTEM.

1st. All these systems, as far as organization is concerned, govern and perpetuate their church life from within, or, in other words, they work organically on very much the same general lines ; whereas Congregationalism is a totally different system, working on totally different lines—lines that exist, because drawn in actual organic opposition to the lines of working pursued by the three great systems of Episcopacy, Presbytery and Methodism. These three systems perpetuate their ministry from the ministry—Episcopacy by bishops, Presbyterianism by presbyters, and Methodism by the joint action of appointed clergy; whereas Congregationalism, judged by its system, perpetuates its ministerial life from without, through the ordination of the congregation itself, or the delegated powers of the congregation. In the three systems, the minister gathers the congregation, in Congregationalism, the congregation gathers the minister, the deposit or gift to be passed on lies not in the ministry but in the congregation. And this very difference, however locally it may be departed from, is one of the fundamental characteristics of Congregationalism, and hence raises an obstacle at once in the way of an initial movement.

2. Each of the three systems naturally moves as an organized body. This is very evident in Canada, where the Provincial Synods of the Church of England, govern all churches in a province, the General Assembly of the Presbyterian Church all churches in every Presbytery; and the Great Conference of Methodism all churches in every circuit. These three systems move organically; and a message or law from headquarters, governs the action of all loyal to headquarters. But Congregationalism, as a system, is fundamentally and practically the very opposite of all this. Each separate congregation, irrespective of age, size, or government, is a whole, entire, and perfect church ; as perfect, as the whole system of Episcopacy, or Methodism. Each congregation is in itself perfect, as a source of law and doctrine. Hence, the Congregational Union of England, finally

established in 1871, lays down as a fundamental
principle of its existence, that it recognizes the right
of each individual church to administer its affairs free
from external control, and that it shall not, as a
Union, in any case, assume legislative authority, or
become a Court of Appeal.

3rd. The three great systems have their distinctive
and clearly expressed rules of faith. The Church of
England in Canada, the three Creeds, the Prayer
Book, the thirty-nine Articles of Religion and the
Catechism. The Presbyterian Church, the Westminster Confession, the larger and shorter Catechisms,
and the Apostles Creed, regarded as a " brief sum-
ming up of the Christian faith agreeable to the Word
of God, and anciently received in the Churches of
God." The Methodist Church, the twenty-five Articles
of Religion (almost identical with the thirty-nine
Articles of the Church of England) the fifty-two
sermons of Wesley, and the Notes of Wesley on the
New Testament, and the Catechisms. Thus, a candidate for the ministry of any one of these three
systems, has a clearly defined field of study, and, on
offering himself for ordination, must, if an honest man,
be prepared to preach according to the rule of faith
laid down in the standards of his church. Here again,
Congregationalism is the very reverse of the three
systems. It believes in, (and its very conception of
the church involves) the most unfettered freedom of
conscience and thought on all religious matters. It
rejects wholly, as authorities of faith, the Councils,
Canons and Creeds of the Primitive Church; hold-
ing solely and alone to the individual understanding of

the Word of God. Hence, any congregation may evolve
its own peculiar interpretation of God's Word, and
if needs be, set apart, and ordain its own pastor to in-
struct it. Such pastor, however, in theory at least,
being perfectly free to exercise his gifts according to
his conscience.

Little, therefore, can be expected from the great
Congregational system in any initial movement towards organic union, although the individual efforts of
leading minds connected with the system, or the aid
and approbation of distinct congregations connected
with it, would, if used in favour of the movement, add
materially to its success.

The initiation of a movement for organic union
then, seems to find its most favorable field, in a representative body, taken from the Episcopal, the Presbyterian, and the Methodist systems, meeting together
on equal terms, to think over the possibility of union;
and, in connection with such a possible conference, I
would now proceed to notice wherein these three
systems agree together, on the great leading fundamental doctrines of the Christian faith; leaving
important points of difference for after consideration.
In doing this, I will deal solely with the acknowledged
standards of the three systems, and not with the views
of individuals, however influential, for if a consultation on unity ever takes place, these standards will
necessarily form the basis of such consultation.

It will be seen as an advance is made in the comparison of doctrines common to the three great reformed systems, that though one result of the Reformation was that of rupturing the organic unity of the Church in Great Britain and Ireland, that it is impossible to prove that any one system monopolized the whole truth. Even admitting the claim of Apostolic Succession in the Church of England, consequent on its retention of Episcopacy, it remains questionable as to how far the happy possession of one inestimable gift can make up for the avowed loss of other gifts, possessed by systems that parted from us at the Reformation. Thus, if the Church of England has retained its succession, it freely acknowledges in its Commination Service that it has largely lost its power of disciplining the laity, which discipline adjusted to the needs of the age, has been ever characteristic of the Presbyterian and Methodist churches.

Then on a full comparison of doctrines common to the three great systems, it will be found that those who regarded Apostolic Succession as valueless or of secondary importance, nevertheless retained their grasp of Apostolic doctrines, and through the earnest preaching of these divine doctrines laid the foundations of independent and powerful systems; so that in no sense can it be claimed that a church in succession (such as the Church of England) alone possesses and alone teaches the doctrines of the Apostolic Church. Hence the Anglican in approaching this question of prospective unity should do so with a feeling that he is approaching those with whom he has not only much in common, but those who have gifts to imitate or bestow, whilst the Presbyterian and Methodist should equally feel that they have much in common with the Church of England, and that it has a gift to bestow which might be re-adjusted to meet the demands of unity without injuring its Apostolic value or power.

POINTS OF AGREEMENT.

ON THE BEING OF GOD.

1st. We agree perfectly on the question of " the Being of God," and hence, as one united Body, could make a powerful organic stand against the Atheism, Agnosticism and Materialism of the age.

THE CHURCH OF ENGLAND

teaches " that there is but one living and true God, without body, parts or passions, of infinite power, wisdom and goodness, the Maker and Preserver of all things both visible and invisible." (Article I.)

THE METHODIST CHURCH

teaches, " there is but one living and true God, everlasting, without body or parts, of infinite power, wisdom and goodness, the Maker and Preserver of all things visible and invisible." (Article I.)

THE PRESBYTERIAN CHURCH

enters at much greater length into definitions as to the person and attributes of Deity; but begins thus: " There is but one only living and true God, who is infinite in Being and perfection,—a most pure Spirit, without body, parts, or passions, etc., the alone fountain of all being, etc." (Confess. chap. 2.)

ON THE HOLY TRINITY.

These three systems agree perfectly on the Trinity of the Godhead.

THE CHURCH OF ENGLAND

teaches, "And in the Unity of this Godhead there be three persons, of one substance, power and eternity, the Father, the Son, and the Holy Ghost." (Article I.)

THE METHODIST CHURCH

teaches "And in the Unity of this Godhead, there are three persons, of one substance, power and eternity, the Father, the Son, and the Holy Ghost." (Article I.)

THE PRESBYTERIAN CHURCH

states, " In the Unity of the Godhead, there be three persons, of one substance, power and eternity, God the Father, God the Son, and God the Holy Ghost." (Confess. cap. 2, 3.)

Here then again, as opposed to Arianism and Unitarianism, these three systems re-echo as with one voice, the Catholic faith of the Scriptures, and Nicea.

ON THE DIVINITY AND WORK OF THE LORD JESUS CHRIST.

THE CHURCH OF ENGLAND

teaches, "That the Son, which is the Word of the Father, begotten from Everlasting of the Father, the Very and Eternal God, and of one substance with the Father, took man's nature in the womb of the Blessed Virgin, so that two whole and perfect natures, that is to say, the Godhead and the Manhood, were joined together in one person, never to be divided, whereof is one Christ, very God and very man, who truly suffered, was crucified, dead and buried, to reconcile his Father to us, and to be a sacrifice, not only for original guilt, but also for the sins of men." (Article II.)

THE METHODIST CHURCH

has made Article No. 2 on this subject, a copy of the Article of the Church of England, except that the words " begotten from everlasting of the Father," are omitted.

THE PRESBYTERIAN CHURCH

The teaching of the Presbyterian Church is much more elaborate, entering into the whole work of Christ, as well as his person ; but where the Confession touches the same points, taken up by the Church of England and the Methodist Church, it uses almost the same language, stating, " The Son of God, the second person of the Trinity, being very and eternal God, of one substance and equal with the Father, did take on him man's nature, etc. So that two whole, perfect, and distinct natures, were inseparably joined together, etc. That the Lord Jesus, by his perfect obedience and sacrifice of himself, etc., hath fully satisfied the justice of his Father, and purchased not only reconciliation, but an everlasting inheritance, etc." (Confess. chap. viii.)

Thus, on the vital truths connected with the person, and work of the Lord Jesus Christ, these three systems are one; so much so, that the Presbyterian could sign the Anglican or Methodist Articles, on this point, or they, the Presbyterian. Now, these doctrines, form the root doctrines of our common Christianity, and, therefore, if we are one here, we are one at the very root. And that in the face of the heresy, and infidelity, which would either degrade Christ to the level of a Jewish prophet, or regard him only as a teacher of superior morals, or reject him altogether.

THE HOLY GHOST.

The standards of the three systems teach as follows:

THE CHURCH OF ENGLAND

teaches, " The Holy Ghost proceeding from the Father and the Son, is of one substance, majesty and glory, with the Father and the Son, very and eternal God. (Article V.)

THE METHODIST CHURCH

repeats, verbatim, the language of the 5th Article of the Church of England. (Article IV.)

THE PRESBYTERIAN CHURCH

states, " the Holy Ghost eternally proceeds from the Father and the Son, and is of one substance, power and eternity with both." (Confess. chap. ii.)

We may then say that, on the great subject of the Being of God, the Trinity, and the Persons of the Trinity ; there is no difference whatsoever between these three systems.

ON THE SUFFICIENCY OF THE HOLY SCRIPTURES FOR SALVATION.

A similar comparison of the standard authorities shows that

THE CHURCH OF ENGLAND

teaches, " that Holy Scripture contains all things necessary to salvation, so that whatsoever is not read therein, nor may be proved thereby, is not to be required of any man as an article of faith, or be thought requisite or necessary to salvation." The Article then proceeds to name the books of the Old Testament, and to state " that all the books of the New Testament, as they are commonly believed, we do receive and account them canonical." (Art. VI.)

THE METHODIST CHURCH

The Methodist Article (No. 5) is, (with one exception to be noticed hereafter) almost word for word identical with that of the Church of England.

THE PRESBYTERIAN CHURCH

The Presbyterian Church is much more elaborate in its definition of the Holy Scriptures. It declares the need of Revelation, names the books of the Old and New Testaments, asserts their inspiration by God, and their authority as coming from God through the Holy Spirit, etc. But when it touches on what is stated by the Church of England and the Methodist Church, its teaching is practically identical with both. It states " That the Scriptures contain the whole counsel of God concerning all things necessary for salvation," to which nothing, at any time, should be added, etc. (Confess. chap. 1.)

Here, then again, we are, so far, one. But the Article of the Church of England, and the Presbyterian Confession, each contains a clause which Methodism has wholly dropped, namely, that referring to the Apocryphal or uninspired Books.

THE CHURCH OF ENGLAND

teaches, " That these books, as St. Jerome states, the Church doth read for example of life and instruction in manners, but doth not apply such books to establish any doctrine."

THE PRESBYTERIAN CHURCH

states more fully, " The books commonly called Apocrypha, not being of divine inspiration, are no part of the canon of Scripture, and therefore, are of no authority in the Church of God, nor to be any otherwise approved, or made use of than other human writings.

THE METHODIST CHURCH

makes no allusion to the Apocryphal books.

The controversy as to the value of the Apocryphal books, was a controversy natural to the Reformation period, but there is practically no controversy on the subject to-day, nor need there be any between the two systems that notice them in their standards.

The Presbyterian Church definitely states that, the Apocrypha is not of divine inspiration, and the Church of England clearly implies it. The Presby-

o

terian Church asserts that such books form no part
of the canon of the Scripture, and the Church of
England practically asserts the same thing, by omit-
ting them from the list of canonical books. The
Presbyterian Church asserts that they are of no
authority in the Church of God; and the Church of
England states that, the church does not apply them
to establish any doctrine. The Presbyterian Church
places them on a level with other human writings,
and the Church of England places them in exactly
the same position by stating, " that the church doth
read them for example of life and instruction of
manners." In short, the Confession and Article,
though differently worded, are in practical agreement; but the Methodist Church, using its privilege
of later birth, has, through dropping all mention of
the Apocrypha, opened out before the compilers
of union Articles of Belief, the important question
as to whether it would not be wise to follow its
example ?

THE SACRAMENTS.

Perhaps there is no subject on which Rome is more
divided from Protestantism, than on the question of
the Sacraments. Rome, not only inventing Sacraments, but defining them as visible signs of an invisible
grace instituted for our *justification.* (Cat. Col. Trent,
part ii. Ques. iii.) Hence, at the Reformation, the
question of the Sacraments became the great question
on which the Reformation turned, for Rome had in

practice, if not by definition, linked them, in this way, with justification in the eyes of God, and the doctrine of Justification by faith alone, had been brought to the front by Luther, and other great Reformers, as the sign of "a standing or a falling church." In fact, if Rome's sacramental views be correct, then the Reformation was a huge religious blunder; whereas, if they be erroneous, then the Reformation was the greatest blessing God ever sent his church, as we may well, with gratitude, believe it to have been. As a result of the all important character of the sacramental question, the English Reformation produced two Protestant definitions of a Sacrament, if, indeed, it be right to call them two, for, in truth, they are but one definition, expressed in different language by two churches: the Church of England, and the Church of Scotland, or, as it is now known in this country, the Presbyterian Church.

THE CHURCH OF ENGLAND

defines a Sacrament as an outward and visible sign of an inward and spiritual Grace, given unto us, ordained by Christ himself, as a means whereby we receive the Grace, and as a pledge to assure us thereof. (Catechism.)

It further states, "that Sacraments are sure witnesses and effectual signs of Grace, and God's good will towards us, by the which He doth work invisibly in us, and doth not only quicken, but also strengthen and confirm our faith in Him. (Art. xxv.)

THE PRESBYTERIAN CHURCH

enters much more fully into the subject, but defines Sacraments, as "holy signs and seals of the Covenant of Grace, immediately instituted by God, to represent Christ and his benefits, and to confirm our interests in Him, as also to put a visible difference between those that belong unto the Church and the rest of the world, and solemnly to engage them to the service of God in Christ, according to His Word." (Confess. chap. 27, 1.)

Here then, both churches agree that a Sacrament is instituted by God as a sign of Grace. But then, both churches proceed further in definition.

THE PRESBYTERIAN CHURCH

goes on to state that, "there is in every Sacrament a spiritual relation, or sacramental union, between the sign and the thing signified; whence it comes to pass, that the names and effects of the one are attributed to the other. That the Grace which is exhibited in or by the Sacraments, rightly used, is not conferred by any power in them; neither doth the efficacy of a Sacrament depend upon the piety or intention of him that doth administer it, but upon the work of the Spirit and the word of Institution; which contains, together with a precept authorizing the use thereof, a promise of benefit to worthy receivers. (Confess. chap. xxvii. ii, iii.)

Here, then, the Presbyterian Church agrees thoroughly with the Church of England, that the visible sign is connected with a spiritual Grace, through the Holy Ghost which quickens, and bestowed by the means of the Sacrament on the worthy receiver.

THE METHODIST CHURCH

defines the Sacraments in almost the words used by the Church of England in its xxvth Article, any difference of language arising from the omission of redundant words, and from changing the word " damnation " into " condemnation."

On the great question, then, of the definition of a Sacrament, these three systems are practically one, and equally so in opposition to Rome, inasmuch as they each declare "that there be only two Sacraments ordered by Christ, that is to say, Baptism and the Supper of the Lord.

Now, let us advance a step further on this sacramental question. One of the great troubles in Protestant churches has arisen, not from controversies in connection with standards, but from judging churches by the individual opinions of men connected with them, and sometimes, by distorted and unfair representations of such opinions. Thus, not a few Methodists and Presbyterians believe firmly, that the Church of England teaches Baptismal Regeneration in the sense that Baptism positively converts, in the highest theological sense of the word, and that it does this through its own inherent baptismal power, when administered through the proper medium. Then again, not a few outside of the Church of England believe that it teaches its children that, in the Lord's Supper, they actually receive the veritable body and blood of Christ which once appeared on earth, and lay on the cross, and entered into heaven. Whereas, the fact of the matter is, that, judged by her standards on these very points of baptismal regeneration, and the presence of the Lord in the Holy Communion, the Church of England takes no higher ground than the other systems, and in some respects, her language may be said to fall short of that used by the two other churches.

BAPTISM.

Thus notice how these three systems stand towards each other on the question of baptismal regeneration. 1st:—

THE PRESBYTERIAN CHURCH

teaches that Baptism is a sign and seal of the Covenant of Grace, of engrafting into Christ, of *regeneration*, of remission of sins, etc., (Confess. xxviii. 1.)

It also states that "regeneration is not confined to baptism, or that all that are baptized are undoubtedly regenerated:" but these very reservations imply, that as a rule, regeneration accompanies' baptism. It further asks, in the outlined prayer used in the administration of baptism, "that God would join the inward baptism of the Spirit, with the outward baptism of water, making it to the infant a seal of adoption, remission of sin, regeneration and eternal life." (Directory for Public Worship.)

THE CHURCH OF ENGLAND

teaches that Baptism is a sign of regeneration, or the new birth, whereby they that receive baptism rightly are grafted into the Church. (Art. xxvii). It also states in the catechism that "by baptism we are made children of grace," and in the Baptismal service it announces after the administration of the sacrament that the child baptized " is regenerate, and grafted into the body of Christ's Church."

THE METHODIST CHURCH

teaches that baptism is "a sign of regeneration, or the New Birth." (Art. xvii.)

2nd.—The three systems agree that this sign of

Regeneration, or the new birth, is connected with an inward grace.

THE PRESBYTERIAN CHURCH

teaches that " there is a grace in baptism, and that we should be humbled for our sinful defilement, and our falling short of, and walking contrary to, the grace of baptism," (Larger Cat. 167.)

It further teaches that " the efficacy or grace of baptism is not tied to the moment of time wherein it is administered," implying that if its presence at that moment be not the rule, at least the efficacy, or grace, is possible at the very moment.

It further states that though the efficacy of baptism may not be tied to the moment, " yet, notwithstanding by the right use of this ordinance, the grace provided is not only offered but really exhibited and conferred by the Holy Ghost to such (whether of age or *infants*,) as that grace belongeth to, according to the Counsel of God's own will in His appointed time." (Confess. xxviii.)

THE CHURCH OF ENGLAND

teaches " that they that receive baptism rightly are grafted into the church, the promises of the forgiveness of sins, and of our adoption to be sons of God by the Holy Ghost are visibly signed and sealed, faith is confirmed, and grace increased by virtue of prayer unto God." (Art. xxvii.)

In the office of baptism, prayer is made that those baptized may be " washed and sanctified by the Holy Ghost," that they may " receive the remission of sins by spiritual regeneration," that " the Holy Spirit may be given to them," that " they may be made partakers of the death and resurrection of the Lord Jesus."

THE METHODIST CHURCH

has dropped out of its article on baptism, reference to the grace of baptism, but belief in the grace is proved clearly elsewhere, as in Art. xvi, where it is stated, that "by sacraments, God doth work invisibly in us, and doth not only quicken, but also strengthen and comfort our faith in Him."

The following questions and answers in the Methodist Catechism, No. ii. are still more pointed.

What is the outward or visible sign or form in baptism?
Baptism with water into the name of the Father and of the Son and of the Holy Ghost.
What is the inward and spiritual grace signified?
Our being cleansed from the guilt and defilement of sin, and receiving a new life from and in Christ Jesus.

In Wesley's sermons, accepted as Church Standards, the grace of Baptism is plainly taught, notably in his xviii sermon on the "Marks of the New Birth," where, in an impassioned appeal to those who had fallen from the grace of Baptism, he addresses these words. "And if ye have been baptized, your only hope can be this, that those who were made children of God by baptism, but are now the children of the devil, may yet receive power to become the sons of God, that they may receive again what they have lost, even the spirit of adoption, crying in their hearts "Abba, Father."

3rd. The three systems declare that "Baptism should be administered to children."

THE CHURCH OF ENGLAND

teaches that the "Baptism of young children is in anywise to be retained in the church as most agreeable with the institution of Christ."—(Art. xxvii.)

THE METHODIST CHURCH

teaches "the Baptism of young children is to be retained in

the church (xxvii Art.). That " baptized infants have the outward advantages of the Christian church, and all the spiritual blessings of the covenant are assured to them when they shall comply with the terms of the Gospel." That "Baptism places them in the same relation to the New Covenant, in which infants were placed to the old by the rite of circumcision," hence, they are spoken of, addressed and exhorted as heirs of Gospel privilege (Methodist Catechism, No. 2.) That " all children, by virtue of the unconditional benefits of the atonement, are members of the Kingdom of God, and therefore graciously entitled to Baptism." (Book of Discipline, clause 55.]

THE PRESBYTERIAN CHURCH

teaches "that the children of such as profess the true religion are members of the visible church—(Confess. xxv. 2. Cat. 62) and that " not only those that do actually profess faith in and obedience unto Christ, but also the infants of one or both believing parents are to be baptized." (Confess. xxviii. 4. Cat. 166.)

Here there is an important difference. The Church of England and the Methodist Church teaching the positive right of childhood to the sacrament; a difference, however, that we suppose must often be tided over, in the wide-spread missionary work of the Presbyterian Church amongst the heathen, where, no doubt, cases of widowed mothers, dying in childbirth, must at times occur.

4th. The three systems agree in teaching that in Baptism, children receive blessings of grace.

THE CHURCH OF ENGLAND

Teaches that, in Baptism, children are made "members of

Christ, children of God, and inheritors of the Kingdom of Heaven." (Catechism.)

THE PRESBYTERIAN CHURCH

teaches that " Baptism doth signify and seal our ingrafting into Christ, and partaking of the benefits of the covenant of Grace."—(Shorter Catechism, 94. Confess. xxviii.)

THE METHODIST CHURCH

teaches that baptized children are to be " spoken of, addressed and exhorted, as heirs of Gospel privileges." (Methodist Cat. No. 2.)

As a whole, therefore, it may be fairly claimed that the three systems are in reasonable accord on the all important question of the sacrament of Baptism.

THE HOLY COMMUNION.

(1.) THE CHURCH OF ENGLAND

teaches that the Holy Communion is a Sacrament, an outward and visible sign of an inward and spiritual grace. (Art. xxviii.)

THE PRESBYTERIAN CHURCH

teaches that " the Holy Communion is a Sacrament, or Holy ordinance, instituted by Christ in His Church, an outward and visible sign, signifying an inward and spiritual grace." (Larger Cat. 162.)

THE METHODIST CHURCH

teaches that it is a Sacrament of our Redemption by Christ's death." (Art. xviii.)

(2.) The three systems teach that the Sacrament of the Lord's Supper is a positive means of Grace.

THE CHURCH OF ENGLAND

teaches that the Sacraments "have a wholesome effect or operation," (Art. xxv.) and that through the Lord's Supper, "our souls are strengthened and refreshed," and that Sacraments "are means whereby we receive blessings," (Catechism.) It teaches that "the benefit is great, if, with a true, penitent heart and lively faith, we receive that Holy Sacrament." (Catechism.) That we should ask God to make it to us "the means of grace and heavenly benediction."

THE PRESBYTERIAN CHURCH

is much stronger in its statements. It teaches that "by the working of the Holy Ghost, and the blessing of Christ, Sacraments become effectual means of salvation." (Larger Cat. 161.) that "worthy communicating leads to growth in grace," (Larger Cat. 168.); that communicants who find no present benefit from the Sacrament are to review their preparation, "and wait for the fruits of it in due time." (Larger Cat. 165.) That the Lord's Supper, "unto true believers, is a sealing of all the benefits of the sacrifice of Christ unto their spiritual nourishment and growth in Him," (Confess. xxix 1.); that it "renews our strength in our pilgrimage and warfare," (Directory) and that "God is to be thanked for the means of grace in word and Sacrament, and for this Sacrament in particular, by which Christ, and all His benefits, are applied and sealed up unto us." (Directory of Worship.)

THE METHODIST CHURCH

teaches that through Sacraments, as "signs of grace," "God doth work invisibly in us, and doth not only quicken, but also strengthen and comfort our faith in Him." (Art. xvi.) It also teaches that when taken "by the faithful," the Lord's Supper "strengthens and refreshes their souls," that it is "an outward and visible sign of an inward and spiritual grace," (Cat. ii.) and that in such as worthily receive, it has "a wholesome effect or operation." (Art. xvi.)

3rdly. The three systems teach that worthy communicants feed upon the body and blood of Christ, to their spiritual nourishment, and growth in grace.

THE PRESBYTERIAN CHURCH

teaches "they that worthily communicate, feed upon the body and blood of Jesus Christ, to their spiritual nourishment, and growth in grace." (Larger Cat., 168.)

THE CHURCH OF ENGLAND

teaches "that the bread which we break, is a partaking of the body of Christ, and likewise the cup of blessing is a partaking of the blood of Christ." (Art. xxviii.)

THE METHODIST CHURCH

teaches "To those that worthily receive, the bread which we break is a partaking of the body of Christ; and likewise the cup of blessing is a partaking of the blood of Christ." (Art. xviii.)

4th. The three systems, whilst teaching that this feeding is not of an earthly, or literal kind, but wholly spiritual, further teaches that, to the worthy receiver, the body and blood of Christ, are spiritually present.

The three systems teach, that the body and blood of Christ are not corporally present, under the bread and wine in the Lord's Supper.

THE PRESBYTERIAN CHURCH

teaches " the body and blood of Christ, are not corporally or carnally present in, with, or under the bread and wine in the Lord's Supper." (L. Cat., 170.)

THE CHURCH OF ENGLAND

teaches "Transubstantiation (or the change of the substance of the bread and wine) in the Supper of the Lord, cannot be proved by Holy Writ, but is repugnant to the plain words of Scripture, overthroweth the nature of a Sacrament, and hath given occasion to many superstitions." (Art. xxviii.) Also, "that the natural body and blood of our Saviour Christ are in heaven and not here." (Declaration at end of Communion Service.)

THE METHODIST CHURCH

teaches "Transubstantiation (or the change of the substance of the bread and wine) in the Supper of the Lord, cannot be proved by Holy Writ, but is repugnant to the plain words of Scripture, overthroweth the nature of a Sacrament, and hath given occasion to many superstitions." Art. xviii.)

THE PRESBYTERIAN CHURCH

teaches that, although the body and blood of Christ is not corporally present, ''yet they are spiritually present to the faith of the receiver, no less truly and really than the elements themselves are to their outward senses. So, they that worthily communicate, do feed upon the body and blood of Christ in a spiritual manner, yet truly and really." (Larger Cat., 170.) (Confession xxxix, 7.)

THE METHODIST CHURCH

teaches that the body of Christ is given, taken, and eaten in the Supper only after a heavenly and spiritual manner, (Art. xvii.) but that the body and blood of Christ are spiritually received, and taken by the faithful, in the Lord's Supper, to the strengthening and refreshing of their souls. (Cat. No. ii.)

teaches "The body and blood of Christ are verily and indeed taken and received by the faithful in the Lord's Supper." (Catechism.)

A close inspection of these standards on this all important point of controversy, and theological teaching, plainly proves that the three systems agree perfectly on the doctrine of the spiritual presence of the body and blood of Christ to the faithful receiver.

(5). The three systems unite in teaching that the Sacrament was not by Christ's ordinance reserved, carried about, lifted up, or worshipped.

Church of England.—6th rubric, close of Communion office. Declaration at close of Communion office. (Art. xxv, xxviii.)

Presbyterian Church.—Confession, chap. xxix-4.

Methodist Church.—Articles xvi. & xviii.

(6). The three systems agree that the cup should not be denied to the laity, as in the Church of Rome.

Church of England.—Article xxx.

Presbyterian Church.—Confession, xxix-4.

Methodist Church.—Article xix.

(7.) The Church of England and the Presbyterian Church teach " that the wicked, and those that be void of faith, although they may consume the sacred elements in an outward act of Communion, yet, in no wise, are they partakers of Christ. (Ch. of England, Art. xxix, Confession, chap. xxix, 8.) This statement is not made by the Methodist Church, although clearly implied in Articles xvi. & xviii., wherein it is stated, " they that receive unworthily, purchase to themselves condemnation," and that " such as rightly, worthily, and with faith receive, do partake of the body and blood of Christ."

John Wesley's renowned sermon on " the duty of constant communion," with regard to which, fifty-five years after it was written, he says, " Thank God, I have not altered my sentiments in any point therein delivered," is well worthy of notice, as showing how fully his teaching was in accord with the Anglican and Presbyterian Churches, on the subject of the Holy Communion. In this sermon he speaks of the " Grace of the Sacrament." He calls it " the Christian Sacrifice," the food of the Soul," the blessed Sacrament," " the sign of inward Grace," " an assistance to obtain divine blessings," " the blessing and mercy of God," and " one of God's greatest mercies on this side of heaven." He urges that Christians should receive it whenever possible, reminding his hearers that in the Primitive Church, " the Christian Sacrifice " was a constant part of the service of the Lord's Day." He answers, at length, objections arising from fear, or sense of sin, or weakness of faith, etc. It is really a wonderful teaching sermon, and one that any clergyman, of either of the three systems, might preach from his pulpit, and yet remain in strict accord with the standards of his church.

Here then, on this great subject, where, judging by the common talk, one might expect the widest disagreement, there is something approaching a wondrous unanimity. A blessed thought, for if ever Ephraim and Judah come together within the folds of the old Patriarchal tent, it is round this holy feast they must come. For consummated unity, means:—one table of the Lord, one service which all may take part in, and one food on which all may feed. To which blessed consummation may the Good Lord bring us all, for the sake of Him who died, and who, with the shadow of death stealing over him, prayed—" that they all may be one."

ON THE "CHURCH" AND CHURCH AUTHORITY.

We now have reached a question on which, if we lay aside standards, and depend on controversies, and opinions of individual men, the three systems would appear hopelessly divided : namely, the Visible Church and its powers. But, our hope of unity lies in a realization of the teaching of these standards, which, after all said or done in the matter, are the authoritative voices of the three systems, and should be regarded as final.

THE CHURCH OF ENGLAND

teaches belief in "the Holy Catholic Church" (Apostles Creed) in "one Catholic and Apostolic Church," (Nicene Creed), in "the Church of God " (ordering of Priests), "the Church of Christ" (consecration of Bishops), "the body of Christ's Church," "the congregation of Christ's flock," (Baptismal Service), "the Church built on the foundation of Apostles and prophets," (Collect St. Simon), "the Holy Church," (Collect St. Mark), God's "Household, the Church," (Collect 22nd Trin.)

(2). It defines the Visible Church of Christ as " a congregation of faithful men, in which the pure Word of God is preached, and the Sacraments be duly administered according to Christ's ordinance in all those things that of necessity are requisite to the same." (Article xix.)

THE METHODIST CHURCH

teaches (1) belief in "the Visible Church of Christ," the "Holy Church," (Catechism ii), the "Holy Catholic Church," (Catechism), "God's Ancient Church," "Christ's Holy Church" "Congregation of Christ's flock," (Baptismal Service), "the Household of God," "the Church our Saviour has purchased with his own blood," "the Church of God," the "Church Militant," (office of reception of members), "the Spouse and Body of Christ," (Ordination Service).

(2). It defines the Church of Christ in the language of the Article of the Church of England, as a "congregation of faithful men, in which the pure Word of God is preached, and the Sacraments duly administered, according to Christ's ordinance, in all those things that of necessity are requisite to the same." (Art. xiii.)

THE PRESBYTERIAN CHURCH

teaches (1) belief in "the Holy Catholic Church (Apostles Creed), "the Catholic or Universal Church," "the Visible Church," "the Kingdom of the Lord Jesus Christ," "the House and family of God."

(2). It defines the church as invisible and visible—the invisible (which is Catholic or Universal) consists of "the whole number of the elect that have been, are, or shall be, gathered into one, under Christ the head thereof; and is the spouse, the body, the fullness of Him that filleth all in all." The visible church, which " is also Catholic or Universal, under the Gospel, and not confined to one nation, as before, under the law, consists of all those throughout the world, that profess the true religion, together with their children, out of which there is no ordinary possibility of salvation." "Unto

D

this Catholic visible Church, Christ hath given the ministry, oracles, and ordinances of God, for the gathering and perfecting of the saints in this life, to the end of the world, and doth by his own presence and spirit, according to his promise, make these effectual thereunto." " Particular churches, which are members of this Catholic Church, are more or less pure, according as the doctrine of the Gospel is taught and embraced, ordinances administered; and public worship performed more or less purely in them." (Confession cap. xxv.) 1,2, 3, 4.)

THE CHURCH OF ENGLAND

after defining the church in its 19th Article, goes on to state, "As the Churches of Jerusalem, Alexandria and Antioch (the Eastern Churches) have erred, so also, the Church of Rome hath erred, not only in their living and manner of ceremonies, but also in matters of faith." This, perhaps, is the most Protestant clause in all the Articles of the Church of England, as it protests, not only against the errors of Rome, but the errors of the Eastern branch of the original church.

THE PRESBYTERIAN CHURCH

does not name these erring churches, but it, no doubt, refers specially to them, and if not, certainly includes them in the xxvth chapter of the Confession, 5th clause, where it says in scorching language: " The purest churches under heaven are subject both to mixture and error, and some have so degenerated as to become no churches of Christ, but synagogues of Satan."

With regard to the authority and discipline of the Church, the three systems teach as follows:—

THE METHODIST CHURCH

states, " that it is not necessary that rites and ceremonies should in all places be the same, and may be changed, etc.

provided nothing be ordained against God's Word. " Whoso-
ever, through his private judgment, willingly and purposely
doth openly break the rites and ceremonies of the Church
to which he belongs, which are not repugnant to the Word of
God, and are ordained and approved by common authority,
ought to be rebuked openly, that others may fear to do the
like, as one that offendeth against the common order of the
church, and woundeth the consciences of weak brethren."
(Art. xxii.)

According to the administration of Methodist discipline,
ministers, and probationers for the ministry, may be tried by
the church, for non-payment of debts, for pursuing secular
business at the expense of spiritual work, for the dissemina-
tion of erroneous doctrine, or for persistently imprudent
conduct.

When a local preacher fails in business, or contracts debts
which he is not able to pay, the superintendent shall appoint
three members of the church to inspect the accounts, contracts
and circumstances of the supposed delinquent, and if in their
opinion he has behaved dishonestly, or contracted debts without the probability of paying, he shall be suspended, till further action be taken. Local preachers can be also tried for
imprudent conduct.

Ordinary lay members may be tried for immoral conduct,
for dissensions, for dishonest failures in business, for non-
payment of just debts, for neglect of duties of any kind
imprudent conduct, indulging in sinful tempers, or words,
buying, selling or using intoxicating drinks as a beverage,
dancing, playing at games of chance, attending theatres,
horse-races, circuses, dancing parties, or patronizing dancing
schools, or taking such other amusements as are obviously
of a misleading or questionable moral tendency, or dis-
obedience to the order and discipline of the church." The
discipline of the laity takes the form of (1). on first offence,
private reproof. (2,) On second offence, inquiry before one or
two faithful friends, (3) On third offence, the case should be
brought before the society, or a select number, and if there be

no sign of real humiliation, the offender must be cut off, (Administration of Discipline, p. 129.) Special courts are organized for the discipline of ministers, and in the case of local preachers, if they be found guilty and impenitent, they shall be expelled from the church, subject, however, to the decision of a court of appeal, if appeal be demanded. After such form of trial and expulsion, such person shall have no privilege of society or sacrament in the church, without contrition, confession and trial (Administration of Discipline, p. 132).

THE PRESBYTERIAN CHURCH

teaches that "the Lord Jesus, as King and Head of the Church, hath therein appointed a government, in the hand of Church officers, distinct from the civil magistrate. To these officers, the keys of the kingdom of heaven are committed, by virtue whereof they have power respectively to retain and remit sins, to shut the kingdom of heaven against the impenitent, both by word and censures, and to open it to penitent sinners by the ministry of the Gospel, and by absolution from censures, as occasion shall require." "For the better attaining of these ends, the officers of the church are to proceed by admonition, suspension from the sacraments of the Lord's Supper, for a season, and by excommunication from the church, according to the nature of the crime and demerit of the person." (Confession, chap. xxx, clauses 1 and 4).

Further, it provides for the better government of the church through synods, or Councils and states. "It belongeth to synods and councils, ministerially, to determine controversies of faith, and cases of conscience, to set down rules and directions for the better ordering of the public worship of God and government of His church, to receive complaints in cases of mal-administration and authoritatively to determine the same, which decrees and determinations, if consonant with the Word of God, are to be received with reverence and submission, not only for their agreement with the Word, but also for the power whereby they are made, as being an ordinance of God, appointed thereunto in His Word." (Confession, xxxi, 3, 4).

It further states that, " the ruling officers have power authoritatively to call before them any member of the congregation, as they shall see just occasion, to enquire into the knowledge and spiritual estate of the several members, to administer and rebuke, to authoritatively suspend from the Lord's table a person not yet cast out of the church." (Form of Church government, p. 310.)

THE CHURCH OF ENGLAND

teaches " the church hath power to decree rites or ceremonies, and authority in controversies of faith : And yet it is not lawful for the church to ordain anything that is contrary to God's Word written ; neither may it so expound one place of Scripture that it be repugnant to another. Wherefore, although the church be a witness and keeper of Holy Writ ; yet, as it ought not to decree anything against the same, so besides the same ought it not to enforce anything to be believed for necessity of salvation." (Article xx.)

It further states that general councils may not be gathered together without the commandment and will of princes. That such councils may err, and that their ordinances have neither strength or authority, unless it may be declared that they be taken out of Holy Scripture. (Art. xxi.)

It further states " that it appertaineth to the discipline of the church that evil ministers, being found guilty, by just judgment, be deposed" (Art. xxvi), and that " a person, who, by open denunciation of the church, is rightly cut off from the unity of the church, and excommunicated, ought to be regarded by the multitude of the faithful as an heathen and publican, until he be openly reconciled by penance, and received into the church by a judge that hath authority thereunto."—(Art. xxxiii.) It also provides " that if any one be an open and notorious evil liver, or have done any wrong to his neighbour by word or deed, so that the congregation be thereby offended, the curate having knowledge thereof shall call him and advertise him that in anywise he presume not to come to the Lord's table until he have truly repented and amended his naughty life, and that he recompense the parties to whom he hath done wrong." "The same order shall the curate use with those betwixt whom he perceiveth malice and hatred to reign, not suffering them to be partakers of the Lord's table until he know them to be reconciled." "And if one of the parties so at variance be content to forgive him from the bottom of his heart, all that the other hath trespassed against him, and to make amends for that he himself hath offended, and that the other party will not be persuaded to a Godly unity, the minister, in that case, ought to admit the penitent person to the Holy Communion, and not him that is obstinate." (Rubric opening of order of Holy Communion.)

According to the administration of discipline in the Chnrch of England in Canada, a bishop may be tried by his peers, (1)for immorality. (2) for false doctrine, (3) for wilful violation of canons of provincial synod, (4) for wilful violation of the canons of his own diocese, the sentence taking the form either of admonition, or suspension, or deposition. Each diocese has its form of trial for erring clergy, resulting, if the accused be found guilty, in admonition, suspension, or deposition. There is no court for the trial of the laity, the only lay discipline being that of partial, or lasting excommunication, for the reasons stated in the rubrics at the opening of the order for the administration of Holy Communion.

In this comparison of the teaching of the three systems on the question of the church and church authority, the definitions of the " visible church " are closely akin, the Anglican and Methodist definitions being identical, the Presbyterian differing only in wording, and a fuller treatment of the subject. On the question of Church authority and the exercise of disci-

pline, all agree ; and on the question of the supreme
authority of the church in dealing with matters of
faith, doctrine and practice, and in the exercise of positive and practical discipline, the Church of England is
left far behind by the two other systems.

ON ABSOLUTION.

It is generally supposed that a vital difference exists
between the three systems on this important subject,
but such an assertion is more easily made than proved,
at least if judged by general principles laid down in
church standards.

THE CHURCH OF ENGLAND

has three forms of absolution. (1) The absolution in morning
and evening prayer; containing (a) a declaration of God's
mercy towards the penitent, (b) of the right of ministers
to pronounce pardon to the penitent, (c) the declaration
that pardon is conditional on penitence and faith, (d) an
admonition to seek for the help of the Holy Spirit. (2) The
absolution in the communion office, which also declares
forgiveness "to all them that with hearty repentance and
true faith turn unto God." (3) The absolution in the order
for the visitation of the sick which dispenses pardon, in
connection with earnest prayer that pardon may be granted.
In this service the clergyman is directed "to move the
sick person to make a special confession of his sins, if
he feel his conscience troubled with any weighty matter.
After which the priest shall absolve him (if he humbly
and heartily desire it) after this sort: Our Lord Jesus Christ,
who hath left power to His church to absolve all sinners
who truly repent and believe in Him, of his great mercy,
forgive thee thine offences. And by His authority com-

mitted unto me, I absolve thee from all thy sins, in the name of the Father, and of the Son, and of the Holy Ghost." Even here, although the mediæval words " I absolve thee," are used, still care is taken to assert that the absolution is conditional on repentance and faith; and that it is the Lord Jesus Christ who forgives—assertions strengthened by the fact, that after the use of the words. ''I absolve thee," the priest immediately proceeds to pray, " that God would look on His servant who desireth pardon and forgiveness, that He would renew in him what had been decayed, that He would consider his tears, that he would not impute unto him his sins."—petitions which alone can mean, that though the personal priestly declaration of forgiveness has been uttered, the actual pardon is in the hands of God. The exhortation to the communion also bids those who cannot quiet their own consciences to come to the curate, or some other discreet and learned minister of God's Word, and open his grief; that by the ministry of God's Holy Word he may receive the benefit of absolution, together with ghostly counsel and advice, to the quieting of his conscience, and avoiding of all scruple and doubtfulness.

THE PRESBYTERIAN CHURCH.

teaches " That the Lord Jesus Christ hath appointed church officers, distinct from the civil magistrates. To these officers, the keys of the kingdom of Heaven are committed, by virtue whereof, they have power, respectively to retain and remit sins : to shut that kingdom against the impenitent, both by word and censures, and to open it unto penitent sinners, by the ministry of the Gospel, and by absolution from censures as occasion may require." (Confess. of Faith, chap. xxx, 1 and 2).

THE METHODIST CHURCH

seems devoid of all teaching by article or standard in connection with the ministerial power of absolution; but the principle of declaratory absolution lies at the very base of Methodism, inasmuch as it declares that the result of every camp and revival meeting is, that so many sinners have been pardoned of their sins and converted to God, and the pardon in the case of erring ministers and local preachers and the laity can only be obtained after confession of sin. (Discipline, p. 132.)

ON JUSTIFICATION BY FAITH.

The doctrine of Justification by Faith as the root doctrine of the Reformation, demands on the part of all favourable to Union, a most careful comparison of church standards, hence the importance of the teaching of the three churches on the subject.

THE CHURCH OF ENGLAND

teaches "That we are accounted righteous before God, only for the merit of our Lord and Saviour Jesus Christ, by faith. and that not for our own works or deservings." It then refers the churchman to the renowned homily, or sermon '·On Justification," for a fuller account of the doctrine based on the lines of the article. (Art. xi.)

It also teaches "that works done before the grace of Christ and the inspiration of His spirit are not pleasant to God, for as much as they spring not of faith in Jesus Christ, neither do they make men meet to receive grace, yea rather, for that they are not done as God hath willed and commanded them to be done, we doubt not but that they have the nature of sin." (Article xiii.)

THE METHODIST CHURCH

teaches "We are accounted righteous before God only for the merit of our Lord Jesus Christ, by faith, and not for our own works or deservings. Wherefore, that we are justified by faith only, is a most wholesome doctrine, and very full of comfort." (Article xi.)

It also has taken the Article xvi of the Church of England, entitled, "Of Sin after Baptism," and reproduced it word for word under an Article headed, "On Sin after Justification." (Article xii.) The Church of England article, reading, "Not every sin willingly committed after *Baptism*, etc.," and the Methodist article, "Not every sin willingly committed after *Justification*, etc." This change, however, does not deny baptismal blessings, as it should be read in the light of the Methodist Article xvi., which states "that in Sacraments, God doth work invisibly in us, and doth not only quicken, but also strengthen and comfort our faith in Him."

The Methodist Church also teaches that remission of sins is "sometimes called Justification," because the forgiven penitent is justified, treated for Christ's sake, as if he were righteous, and that as such he is made inwardly righteous by the renewing of the Holy Spirit, who enables him to do righteousness. (Cat. ii, chap. 3, Q. 3, 4, 5.)

THE PRESBYTERIAN CHURCH

teaches "that those whom God effectually calleth, he also freely justifieth, not by infusing righteousness into them, but by pardoning their sins, and by accounting and accepting their persons as righteous. Not for anything wrought in them, or done by them, but for Christ's sake alone; not by imputing faith itself, or the act of believing or any other evangelical obedience to them, as their righteousness, but by imputing the obedience and satisfaction of Christ unto them, they receiving and resting on him and his righteousness by faith, which faith they have not of themselves, it is the Gift of God." (Confess., chap. xi.) It further teaches that Justification is an act of God's free grace unto sinners, in which He pardoned all their sins, accepteth and counteth their persons righteous in his sight, not for anything wrought in them, or done by them, but only for the perfect obedience and full satisfaction of Christ, by God imputed unto them, and received by faith alone." (Larger Catechism Q. 70.)

Now, this question of Justification is a tremendous central thought for Protestant unity to cluster round. Here, (laying aside for the present the Presbyterian view of election) the three systems are as one on the worth and value of our Lord's death, as an atonement for our sins, and also on the value of personal faith as a Gift of God in that atonement. When, as here, the three systems stand like the disciples and the women about the cross of Christ, looking up to it, trusting in it alone for justification in the sight of God, drawing all spiritual life from it through the "application of Christ's death by the Holy Spirit," and resting safely under its shadow, who could dream that we leave the healing vision on the cross, to pursue our separated paths divided and alone ? "If I be lifted up," said the Saviour, "I will draw all men to me,"— a wondrous promise or prophecy that can never be fulfilled in its perfection until "we all are one."

ON GOOD WORKS.

THE CHURCH OF ENGLAND

teaches " that good works which are the fruits of faith, and follow after Justification, cannot put away our sins, and endure the severity of God's Judgment, yet are they pleasing and acceptable to God in Christ, and do spring out necessarily of a true and lively faith, insomuch that by them a lively faith may be as evidently known, as a tree discerned by the fruit." (Article xiii.)

Also, that "we have no power to do good works pleasant and acceptable to God, without the Grace of God by Christ going before us, that we may have a good will, and working with us when we have that will. (Article x.)

It also prays that grace may be given us " to perceive and know what things we ought to do," (1st collect after Epiphany) " that we may think things that be good, and by God's guidance, may perform the same," (5th after Easter) that " by the help of God's grace we may keep His commandments, and please Him both in will and deed," (1st after Trinity) that God's grace " may go before and follow us, and make us continually to be given to all good works," (17th after Trinity) that " we may be devoutly given to serve God in good works, to the glory of His name," (22 Trinity) that " God would stir up the wills of His faithful people, that they, plenteously bringing forth the fruit of good works, may of God be plenteously rewarded," (25th after Trinity) that like St. Andrew, " we may give ourselves up to fulfil God's commandments," that like St. John the Baptist, " we may constantly speak the truth, boldly rebuke vice, and patiently suffer for the truth's sake," and that " grace may be given us to follow the blessed Saints in all virtuous and godly living, that we may come to those unspeakable joys, which God has prepared for them that unfeignedly love Him, through Jesus Christ our Lord."

THE METHODIST CHURCH

teaches almost word for word the 13th Article of the Church of England, except where it gives a modern use for an old word, as, " although" for " albeit," and also where it omits (no doubt as redundant) the word "necessarily" in the sentence "good works do spring out necessarily of a true and lively faith."

It also teaches that " those who continue in the societies should evidence their desire of salvation by their conduct."

1st. By avoiding evil, swearing, profanation of the Sabbath, drunkenness, etc., fighting and quarrelling, going to law, usury, defrauding the Customs, uncharitable or unprofitable conversation, putting on of gold or costly apparel, etc., etc.

2nd. By doing good; being kind, merciful, charitable. By helping those who are seeking to be good; buying of one another, helping each other in business, etc. By denying self and taking up the cross daily.

3rd. By attending all the ordinances of God (General Rules, sec. iii), and by "contributing of earthly substance, according to ability, to the support of the Gospel, and the various benevolent enterprises of the Church." (Reception of members.)

THE PRESBYTERIAN CHURCH

teaches, in an elaborate article, "good works are the fruits of faith;" that "ability to do them is wholly from the Spirit of Christ;" that "the best fall short of what they ought to do;" that "works cannot merit pardon of sin, or eternal life at the hands of God;" that "nevertheless good works are acceptable to Christ," and that "the works of the unregenerate are sinful and cannot please God." (Confess. chap. xvi.)

It also orders that prayer should be made that Christians should seek for "grace to fit and enable them for all duties of conversation and calling towards God and man, strength to resist temptation, the sanctified use of blessings and crosses; and perseverance in faith and obedience to the end." It also orders that the preacher "should exhort to duties as he seeth cause, to teach also the means that help to a performance of them, to show the danger of special sins, and the best way to avoid them." (Directory for Public Worship.)

A careful comparison of the teaching of these three systems on this all important subject, discloses once again the fact, that for all practical purposes of Christian life, they are in common sense accord.

ON THE DIVINE INSTITUTION OF THE MINISTRY AND CALL THERETO.

THE CHURCH OF ENGLAND

teaches "that it is not lawful for any man to take on himself the office of public preaching, or ministering the sacraments in the congregation, before he be lawfully called and sent to execute the same. And those we ought to judge lawfully called and sent, which be chosen and called to this word, by men who have public authority given them in the congregation, to call and send ministers into the Lord's vineyard." (Article xxiii.)

In the ordering of priests, those about to be ordained are asked, "Do you think in your heart you are truly called?" The priest is ordained by the bishop "to preach the Word of God, and to minister the holy sacraments in the congregation, whereunto he is lawfully appointed." By the Act of Ordination, priests are admitted to "this function and ministry," "this holy ministry," "unto the office of the ministry," to "the order and ministry of the priesthood," to "the office and work of a priest in the Church of God." The candidates are reminded of the "high dignity" and "importance of this weighty office," of "how great a treasure is committed to their charge," and are ordained, kneeling, by the imposition of the hands of the bishop with "those of the priests present," the following words being used: "Receive the Holy Ghost for the office and work of a priest in the Church of God, now committed unto thee by the imposition of our hands, whose sins thou dost forgive, they are forgiven, and whose sins thou dost retain, they are retained. And be thou a faithful dispenser of the Word of God, and of His holy sacraments: in the name of the Father, and of the Son, and of the Holy Ghost. Amen." These words are uttered after the use of the "Veni, Creator Spiritus," in which the Holy Ghost is implored to "inspire the souls," to "lighten with celestial fire," to "anoint with his seven-fold gifts," and to "give his blessed unction from above" to those about to be ordained.

THE PRESBYTERIAN CHURCH

teaches that "Christ hath given the ministry oracles, ordinances of God, for the gathering and perfecting of the saints in this life, to the end of the world; and doth by His own presence and spirit, according to His promise, make them effectual thereunto." (Article xxv. 3.) That "neither sacraments may be dispensed by any but by a minister of the Word lawfully ordained (Confess. xxvii. 4) or lawfully called (xxviii. 2). That "all are not permitted to read the Word publickly to the congregation " (Cat. 156). "That the Word of God is to be preached only by such as are sufficiently gifted, and duly approved and called to that office; and that the charge and office of interpreting the Holy Scriptures is a part of the ministerial calling, which none, however otherwise qualified, should take upon him in any place." (Directions iii, Cat. 158). That "Christ hath appointed the ministers of His Word in the administration of the Lord's Supper " (Cat. 169). That "Christ hath appointed officers for the edification of His Church, to read and preach the Word, to catechise, to dispense Divine mysteries, to administer the sacraments, to bless the people from God, to take care of the poor, and to rule." That " no man ought to take on him the office of minister without a lawful calling, and that every minister is to be ordained by imposition of hands, and prayer, with fasting." (The Form of Church Government.)

In connection with the ordination of ministers, it is ordered that, " on the day appointed for ordination, which is to be performed in that church where he that is to be ordained is to serve, a solemn fast shall be kept by the congregation." After a sermon concerning the office and duty of ministers, the preacher shall, in the face of the congregation, demand of him who is to be ordained, concerning his

faith in Christ, his intentions and ends in entering the ministry, his diligence in his future duties, his faithfulness against
error and schism, his personal and family conduct. After
receiving proper answers and questioning the congregation
as to their readiness to obey and submit to the minister of
Christ, etc., the ministers present solemnly set the candidate
apart to the office and work of the ministry by the imposition
of hands and prayer, imploring "God to fit him with his
Holy Spirit, to fulfil the work of the ministry in all things,
that he may both save himself and the people committed to
his charge." (The form of church government). The actual
words of ordination are not given, but they are implied in
the ordination prayer. No mention is made of the "binding
and loosing" conferred in the act of ordination as performed
in the Church of England, but the power to bind and loose
is plainly stated as connected with the ministerial office, in
the Confession of Faith, in which it is announced that "the
Lord Jesus, as King and Head of his Church, hath appointed a government in the hands of church officers, distinct
from the civil magistrate, and to these officers the keys of
the Kingdom of Heaven are committed, by virtue whereof
they have power respectively to retain and remit sins, to
shut that kingdom against the impenitent both by the word
and censures, and to open it unto penitent sinners by the
ministry of the Gospel, and by absolution from censures as
occasion shall require" (Confession, Chap. xxx).

THE METHODIST CHURCH

has no distinct article on the subject of the ministry, but
that the ministry is a distinct order separate from the laity,
and that none should minister apart from a divine call is
plainly taught in the doctrine and discipline of the Methodist
Church.

The existence of the ministry as a distinct class is taken
for granted in the "Rules of the Society," in the "Basis of
Union," and throughout the whole of the discipline of the

Church. Those about to be ordained are examined as to whether they think "they are moved by the Holy Ghost to preach." The minister is constituted by the election of the annual conference and is set apart by the laying on of hands, "to conduct all parts of Divine service, to administer Baptism and the Lord's Supper, to solemnize matrimony, etc." By the act of ordination, the candidates are admitted "into this function and ministry," "this sacred ministry," "into the office of the ministry," "into the office and work of a minister in the Church of God." They are reminded of "the high dignity and importance of this weighty office," of "how great a treasure is committed to their hands," and are ordained kneeling, by two, or more ministers, the following words being used :—

"The Lord pour upon thee the Holy Ghost for the office and work of the ministry in the Church of God now committed unto thee by the imposition of our hands. And be thou a faithful dispenser of the Word of God, and of his holy sacraments, in the name of the Father and of the Son and of the Holy Ghost, Amen." These words are uttered after the use of the "Veni, Creator Spiritus," in which the Holy Ghost is implored to inspire the souls, to lighten with celestial fire, to anoint with his seven-fold gifts and to give his blessed unction from above to those about to be ordained.

It is plain from the foregoing comparison that the three systems are agreed (1), on the Divine Institution of the Ministry; (2), on its being, as an order, distinct from the laity; (3), on the necessity of a proper call and transmission of authority; (4), on the duties of the ministerial office; (5), on its dignity, responsibility and honour; (6), on the power of the ministry to bind and loose and to excommunicate and declare absolution. The binding and loosing and excommunicatory powers of the Methodist ministry

E

may bo found in the comparison of the teaching of the three systems, on "the Church." (page 50).

ON FASTING.

The teaching on this subject is well worthy of consideration, as a comparison of standards disposes of some popular accusations brought against the Church of England.

THE PRESBYTERIAN CHURCH

teaches " that solemn fastings are in their several times and seasons to be used in a holy and religious manner," (Confession, xxi : 5) that religious fasting is a duty arising out of obedience to the second commandment. (Larger Cat. 108.)

It further teaches that religious fasting requires total abstinence from food except in cases of bodily weakness from bodily labour, etc. That it should be used in times of public judgments, or when some special blessing is to be sought and obtained. That besides general fasts enjoined by authority, congregations may keep days of special fasting, and that families may do the same, etc., (Directory for Public Worship), and that " upon the day appointed for ordination, which is to be performed in that church where he that is to be ordained is to serve, a solemn fast shall be kept by the congregation," etc. (Form for ordination, etc).

THE METHODIST CHURCH

teaches " that fasting or abstinence is required of those who desire to continue in these societies" (General Rules 43), that ministers and probationers should use as much abstinence and fasting every week as their health, strength and labour will permit. (Of the Ministry, Sec. iii 199 : 4.) Ministers are warned against being enthusiasts, looking for the end without using the means, and, amongst other practical questions, should ask themselves : " Do we know the obliga-

tion and benefit of fasting or abstinence ? How often do we
practice it ? The neglect of this alone is sufficient to account
for our feebleness and faintness of spirit. We are continually grieving the Holy Spirit of God by the habitual neglect
of a plain duty. Let us amend from this hour." (219). In
Wesley's standard sermon (No. xxvii), he notices how the
Pharisee used all the means of grace and that our righteousness should exceed his. He then proceeds to ask the following questions : " Do you go as far as he did? Do you fast
much and often ? Twice in the week ? I fear not. Once at
least ; on all Fridays in the year ? (So our church clearly
and peremptorily enjoins all her members to do; to observe
all these, as well as the vigils and the forty days of Lent, as
days of fasting or abstinence.) Do you fast twice in the
year ? I am afraid some among us cannot plead even this."
" If thy labour and bodily strength will not allow of thy
fasting twice in the week—deal faithfully with thine own
soul, and fast as often as thy strength will permit." In
Sermon xxix, he shows (1), what is the nature of true fasting—namely, not to eat; (2), the grounds and reasons and
ends of fasting. (a), sorrow ; (b) a sense of sin ; (c) a sense
of abuse of food ; (d), the punishment of the body ; (e), as
a help to prayer ; (f), to avert the wrath of God, as shown
by the heathen, by kings, by prophets, by apostles, (3) Fasting as a means appointed by God to gain temporal blessings,
to draw out obedience and to obtain rewards ; (4), the objections against fasting, such as (a), fast from sin not from food ;
(b), fast from besetting sins ; (c), we have fasted much, but
obtained no benefit ; (d) God will not notice such little
things ; (e), why not fast always ; (f), use Christian temperance. (5), How to fast. (a), For God's glory ; (b), apart from
a sense of merit ; (c), not to the detriment of the body, but
with (a), application of soul ; (b), with prayer ; (c), with
alms giving. (Wesley's Sermons' xxvii).

THE CHURCH OF ENGLAND

teaches that certain days of fasts and abstinence should be

observed in the year. They are divided into five classes. (1), the forty days of Lent ; (2), the four Ember days, when supplication is made for those about to be ordained ; (3), the three days preceding Ascension Day, called Rogation Days ; (4), all the Fridays in the year, except Christmas Day ; (5), the eves or vigils before certain festivals.

ON DIRECTING THE CONGREGATION IN PUBLIC PRAYER.

At first sight one might fancy that this subject would come naturally under the head of "Points of Difference" between the three systems, but a careful study of standards, leads one to realize that although liturgies may not be common to each, the principle of directing public worship is the property of all. In an actual liturgy, we possess the very words which are used in worship, as in the Roman Mass, or the Book of Common Prayer ; but such an arrangement of words arises from the great underlying principle, that the church should guide the public devotions of the people. The full development of this principle would give us written prayers for all public occasions, its partial development, specially prepared forms for special occasions, and its arrested development, topics of prayer, so fully described as almost to amount to a form of sound words. The "Bidding Prayer" of the Church of England is a type of the "arrested development" of a form of prayer : the people being only bid on to pray on certain topics, but it is not uncommonly used as a prayer in cathedrals and collegiate congregations in England and elsewhere. A careful study of the three systems, in connection with their modes of public worship, discloses these three phases of the great principle, that in some sense, it is the duty of the church to guide, either by word or topic, the public devotions of the people.

THE PRESBYTERIAN CHURCH.

In the Presbyterian Church, we possess a clear case of "the arrested development" of a form of words. In 1560, the liturgy of John Knox, modelled on the Genevan liturgy, was adopted by the Act of the General Assembly as the established form of worship and remained in use until the year 1645, so that, for eighty-five years after the Reformation, the Presbyterian Church of Scotland was a liturgical church. Then, the force and power of an actual liturgy was arrested by the adoption of the Directory of Public Worship, which guides the worship of the Presbyterian Church world over to-day.

This Directory of Public Worship aimed at obtaining a measure of uniformity in worship in all churches, not by publishing words of prayer, but "the general heads, the sense and the scope of the prayers and other parts of public worship." This was done for the direction of ministers in their administrations, to aid them in "keeping like soundness in doctrine and prayer," and "if needs be," to give them "some help and furniture," and yet, in such a way as to prevent them "becoming slothful and negligent in stirring up the gifts of Christ in them, etc." In other words, the Directory furnished the leading topics for prayer, its outlined petitions, leaving it to the minister to use his own discretion, as to the words in which he would clothe the sacred thoughts put into his mind by the wisdom of the church. In fact, the Presbyterian Church gave the godly man who possessed the gift of language, the "help and furniture" of thought.

The Directory consists of a series of directions for worship, and of extended outlines of prayer. The directions begin with the conduct of the congregation on assembling, and follow the service until the congregation is dismissed with the blessing. The prayers are outlined "in extenso," as in the public prayer before the sermon, where the outlined petitions, if turned into a prayer and read or delivered with a reverential utterance, would take up a much longer period of time than the Litany of the Church of England inclusive of all the additional prayers commonly used in connection with it. The direction, at the close of this prayer, allows the minister liberty of deferring some of the petitions till after his sermon, but it plainly implies, that the church expects that all the petitions will be used in some part of public worship.

In the "Directions of the General Assembly concerning secret and private worship," a step in advance of authorized outlined prayers is taken ; a set form of prayer being allowed under certain conditions. "So many as can conceive prayer, ought to make use of that gift of God ; although those who are rude and weaker may begin at a set form of prayer, but so as they be not sluggish in stirring up in themselves (according to their daily necessities) the spirit of prayer," etc. The "rude and sluggish," are then told to pray for the gift of prayer, and in the meantime for their greater encouragement, materials of prayer are given them to meditate on. (1). "To confess unworthiness, etc. (2). To confess sins. (3). Ask for forgiveness. (4). Give thanks to God for mercies. (5). Pray for particular needs. (6). Pray for those in church and state, for friends present and absent. (7). Close with an ascription of Glory to God."

In the administration of Baptism, the minister is directed to use words of instruction, touching the institution, nature, ends of the sacrament, the thoughts from which such words would spring, being given him at length. He is further instructed to admonish the baptized to look back on their baptism, to exhort the parents to bring up the child properly, and that prayer is also to be joined to the words of institution, for "sanctifying the water to this spiritual use," asking God to "join the inward baptism of his Spirit with the outward baptism of water, and to make the baptism to the infant, a seal of adoption, remission of sin, regeneration and eternal life, and all other promises of the covenant of Grace." Directions are then given for the administration of the sacrament, the actual words being furnished and choice given between pouring and sprinkling of water. A form of thanksgiving prayer is then outlined, and further supplication made for the child, as "a member of the household of faith, and as a partaker of Christ's "inestimable benefits."

In the administration of "the Communion or Sacrament of the Lord's Supper," the fullest directions are given as to the mode of administration, etc., and the service taken part in by the minister is fully outlined. He is to exhort the communicants on the inestimable benefit of the sacrament, and its ends and use, to warn the wicked from the table and invite the penitent, to sanctify and bless the elements by the words of Institution and prayer, and to break the bread and hold the cup whilst using the Divine words. After all have communicated, the minister is to remind the communicants "of the Grace of God in Jesus Christ, held forth in this sacrament, and exhort them to walk worthy of it, and also to give solemn thanks to God for the sacramental mercies and goodness vouchsafed."

The solemnization of Marriage is ordered to be observed in the place of public worship, and the general marriage service is outlined for the minister. He is to (1) acknowledge sin and its bitterness. (2). How the Lord will "be the portion," etc., of those about to be married. (3). He is then to declare to them out of Scripture, the institution, use, and ends of marriage, exhorting them to contentment, etc. (4) After enquiring as to impediments, etc., "he shall cause—first, the man to take the woman by the right hand, saying these words :—

"I, N——, do take thee N—— to be my married wife, and in the presence of God, and before this congregation, promise and covenant to be a loving and faithful husband unto thee, until God shall separate us by death ;" and then the woman goes through the same form. (5). Then, without further ceremony, " the minister shall, in the face of the congregation, pronounce them to be husband and wife, according to God's ordinance," and conclude the service with a prayer, which is outlined.

It is clear from the foregoing extracts, that whilst the Presbyterian Church uses in her service free prayer instead of written prayer, that it fashions and moulds the thoughts of free prayer, guiding with scrupulous care and wisdom, the devotions of the people.

THE METHODIST CHURCH.

In the Methodist Church we possess a case where the church authorizes both Liturgical and Free Prayer, a marked step in advance of the Presbyterian Church towards a settled liturgy. The rules directing Public Worship assume that prayer will be extemporary, but the Lord's Prayer is ordered to be used on all occasions of public worship in concluding the first prayer, and the Apostolic benediction in dismissing the congregation. (Discipline, p. 38.) Under the head of "The Ritual of the Church," are forms of service for ; (1) The Baptism of infants and adults. (2) Reception of members. (3) For the administration of the Lord's Supper. (4) For Marriage. (5) Form for burial of the Dead. (6) Form of Ordaining Ministers. (7) Form for Renewing the Covenant. (8) Form for Laying the corner stone of a Church. (9) Form for the Dedication of a Church. In this Ritual, the Order of Service for Baptism, and the Lord's Supper, and the forms for Marriage, Burial and Ordination, are all taken from like services in the ritual of the Church of England. It is here well worthy of notice that whilst extemporary prayer is made the rule of public service, that the highest act of Divine

Worship—the Holy Communion,—is liturgical, as also the great foundation service of the church that of Holy Baptism.

THE CHURCH OF ENGLAND.

The service of the Church of England is wholly liturgical, not only in " The Order for Morning and Evening Prayer," but in the Sacramental and occasional offices. The ordinary service of the old British church was derived through the Gallican liturgy, from the Ephesine use, and not from the Roman (Palmer's Antiquities of Primitive Liturgies), a fact which led Augustine, under the direction of Gregory, to give to the English Church, its own national use, founded on the Roman and Gallican models, which use gave rise to, the uses of York, Sarum, Hereford, Exeter, Lincoln and Aberdeen, the use of Sarum, (Salisbury) being the most popular. In 1516, and again in 1542 (Henry VIII.) revised editions of the Sarum Breviary were published, in 1543 the reading of Scripture was made compulsory, and in 1544 the liturgy was revised by Cranmer, and set forth for public use. In 1547 (Edward VI.) the Book of Homilies, or Sermons providing Scriptural instruction for the people were issued by Royal authority, and the Epistle and Gospel for the day directed to be read in English. In 1548, an English form of Communion, added to the Latin Mass, was published by Royal authority, restoring the cup to the laity, and changing " the Mass " into " the communion," and the next year, the Book of Common Prayer, or " First Prayer Book of Edward," was sanctioned by convocation and accepted by Parliament, thus giving the Church of England but one use, which by the Act of Uniformity (2 and 3, Ed. VI. c. 1, Jan. 15, 1549), was ordered to be said and used in all congregations, with certain qualifications for the benefit of scholars. In this prayer book, morning and evening prayer began with the Lord's Prayer, and ended with the third collect, the litany appeared as a distinct service ; the Communion service began with a psalm, and the Commandments were not read, but the whole book was distinctly Anglican, being a version of the old service books of the English Church. (Proctor 28.) As the spirit of Reformation proceeded, the influence of Bucer and Martyr, who had been appointed to the Divinity chairs of the two Universities. became apparent, the demand for further alteration being freely made, leading finally to the publication of the second Prayer Book of Edward, in 1552, the Act of Uniformity passing both houses of parliament on the 6th of April. In the reign of Mary, the Acts of Uniformity. passed in the reign of Edward, were repealed, but on the accession of Elizabeth, the repeal was reversed, and the second Book of Edward, slightly changed, was brought into legal use. Upon the accession of James I. (1603) the King acceded to the request of the Puritans for a conference, which was held at Hampton Court, after which the book was again revised, in which state it remained until the Restoration, when, at the request of the Presbyterians, the King consented to a fresh revision, (1661) resulting, after the Savoy Conference, in the present Prayer Book, which was adopted by convocation in 1662, and confirmed by Act of Parliament.

THE CHURCH OF ENGLAND IN CANADA.

The Church of England in Canada, as an integral part of the Church of England, states, in its Declaration of Principles, " we recognise the true canon of Scripture, as set forth by the Church of England, on the testimony of the primitive Catholic Church, to be the rule and standard of faith. We acknowledge the Book of Common Prayer and Sacraments, together with the Thirty-nine Articles of Religion, to be a true and faithful declaration of the doctrines contained in the Holy Scripture, etc., etc."

In the 13th canon of the Provincial Synod, the possibility of further revision is provided for as follows. " No alteration or addition shall be made in the Book of Common Prayer and Administration of the Sacraments and other rites and ceremonies of the church, the Articles of Religion or the Form and Manner of making, ordaining and consecrating bishops, priests and deacons, or the version of the Scripture authorized to be read in churches, unless the same shall be enacted at one session of the Provincial Synod, and confirmed at another session of the same; provided that the confirmation be approved by two-thirds of the House of Bishops, and two-thirds of each order of the Lower House." " Nevertheless, any alteration in, or addition made to the Prayer Book, or Articles by the (Mother) Church of England in her convocations, and authorized by Parliament, may be accepted for use in this Ecclesiastical Province by the Provincial Synod, at one Session only, without the necessity for further confirmation."

By canon xii, of Provincial Synod, a shortened form of Morning and Evening Prayer " is allowed to be used on week days under the written sanction of the Bishop." Special forms for special occasions, are also allowed, and a sermon may be preached, at any time, provided a collect and the Lord's Prayer be used.

From the foregoing facts, it appears plain that the three systems agree on the great principle that the church should guide the devotions of the people. They differ as to the extent of that guidance, but the difference is not of that nature which shuts out all possibility of united action, arising out of prayerful and brotherly consultation for God's glory and the welfare of His church.

It is not necessary to enter at length into the many other Articles of Belief common to either two or three of the great Protestant systems, and more or less harmoniously taught in their various standards; but the following list of Articles of a common faith, when added to those already described, seems to exhaust largely the general faith of reformed Protestant Churches :—

Article of Faith.	Teaching of Church of England.	Teaching of Methodist Church.	Teaching of Presbyterian Church.
1. The Resurrection of Christ	Article IV.	Article III.	Conf. VIII. 4,
2. The Old Testament	" VII.	" VI.	" 1-2-7, VIII. 6, XI. 6, XIX. 3.
3. Original Sin	" IX.	" VII.	" VI. 3-4.
4. The One Oblation of Christ on the Cross	" XXXI.	" XX.	" VIII. 5.
5. Eternal Punishment	Athanasian Creed, Commination Service, Litany, Catechism, Homilies.	Wesley's XV. Sermon. Cat. 2, cap. X. 10-13.	" XXXII. 2. XXXIII. 2.
6. Free-Will	Article X.	Article VIII.	" IX. 3-4.
7. Purgatory, Worship of Images, etc.	" XXII.	" XIV.	" XXXII. 1, Cat. 109.
8. The Evil of the Romish Mass	" XXXI.	" XX.	" XXIX. 2.
9. Ministering in an Unknown Tongue	" XXIV.	" XV.	" XXXI. 3.
10. Celibacy of Clergy	" XXXII.	" XXI.	" XXII. 7.
11. Christian Men's Goods	" XXXVIII.	" XXIV.	" XXIV. 3.
12. A Christian Man's Oath	" XXXIX.	" XXV.	" XXVI. 3.
13. The Observance of great Church Festivals	Collect, Gospel and Epistle for each Festival.	"Always avail yourself of the Great Festivals by preaching on the occasion." Discipline, p. 101.	" XXII. 2.

POINTS OF DIFFERENCE BETWEEN THE THREE SYSTEMS.

CHURCH GOVERNMENT.

The crucial point of difference between the three systems, really lies in the question of the government of the church. No one can approach the subject from any standpoint, without feeling its importance, and the necessity of entering upon its discussion with a generous and brotherly spirit, as different from the spirit of of Savoy, or Hampton Court, as light could be from darkness. In no sense can the discussion be avoided, for if ever union comes, it must be union under one government, all other ideals of union being sentimental and evanescent in their nature. The fact, however, of the discussion (if it should occur) taking place in Canada, under the conditions of religious life characteristic of this country, is largely in its favour. Here, as far as the Anglican and Methodist Churches are concerned, it cannot be said, that the " church is the clergy," for both churches agree to the full, with what some Presbyterian divines claim to be the peculiar characteristic of Presbyterianism, " that the church is more than the clergy," and that " the people have a right to share in its government." In the Anglican Church of Canada the people have an equal voice with the clergy, from voting one dollar in vestry up to the election of a bishop, or the passing of canons touching the most important theological doctrines. No candidate for Holy Orders can be ordained without the consent of the laity. As a rule, appointments to parishes are made, in some way, subject to their approbation, and no committee on any really important church movement could hope for success in its work unless the laity were largely represented on it. In the Methodist Church, the laity are entitled to take part in the Government of the church, if not to the full extent characteristic of the Church of England, at least to that extent which makes them part and parcel of the church in the strictest sense of the term. Then, as far as the Church of England in Canada is concerned, its bishops are such, apart from all of the objections most unjustly raised against the Episcopate in England. They form no integral part of the Legislature of the country and their incomes are the least that they could receive, when compared with the natural expenses of their position. As a rule, the bishops consecrated in Canada have no legal right to special titles of honour, receiving them simply as acts of courtesy they have no more power in their various synods as representatives of an order, than the order of the clergy, or order of the laity; for if a bishop can veto the will of the laity and clergy exercising their right of voting by orders, either order can veto any resolution brought before the synod by a bishop, as a representative of his order. No missionary could work harder than the missionary bishops of the Canadian Church, and, in one sense, nearly all the Canadian bishops may be regarded as Missionary Bishops, inasmuch as the wildest and roughest districts lie within the bounds of their respective dioceses.

But these advantages, however they may diminish the difficulties of approaching the question of a united government, do not really touch it, nor would it be wise for any individual, at the present stage of the question, to broach his personal views, and, through doing so, run the dangerous risk of being regarded by some as the mouthpiece of the church to which he might happen to belong. But, as of old, the Spirit of the living God "moved on the face of the waters," bringing order out of chaos, so might God's children reasonably expect, that if the representatives of the scattered portions of His once united church met together, and, with chastened hearts, prayed for the Holy Spirit to lead them on this and other questions His guidance would, in some measure, surely be theirs. And if His guidance were vouchsafed, who would dare to limit the power of His presence, or its consequences to the rent and torn church of God. If once that guidance welded unto one, " Parthians and Medes and Elamites, and dwellers in Mesopotamia." and brought into living unity the ever-growing church of Christ, one need not be hopeless of such a guidance, even now. But all rests with God. Neither wisdom, nor learning, nor the skill of man in debate, or consultation, will settle a question such as this. All such gifts will prove admirable instruments, if used by God, but apart from the Spirit's guidance, will be but " as the battle of the warrior, confused with noise, and garments rolled in blood." Our sole and only hope and trust, can be found in God's Holy Spirit, "giving us grace to lay to heart the great dangers we are in through our unhappy divisions, taking away from us all hatred, and prejudice, and whatever else may hinder us from Godly union and concord, enabling us to realize the one Body, the one Spirit, the one Faith, the one Baptism, the one God and Father of us all, so that we may henceforth long and pray for the one heart, and one soul, which would unite us in one holy bond of Truth and Peace, of Faith and Charity, and lead us with one mind and one mouth to glorify God, through Jesus Christ our Lord."

THE ORDINATION OF MINISTERS.

It is necessary, however, for the general direction of public thought, and to disabuse the public mind of many wide-spread mistakes, to bring together the teaching of the standards of the three systems on the subject of Ordination. And in doing this, the mode hitherto adopted will be pursued, namely, that of clinging to church standards and passing over the opinions and glosses of individuals.

THE CHURCH OF ENGLAND.

The Church of England in Canada teaches :—

" As members of the Church of England, we maintain the form of church government by bishops, priests and deacons, as Scriptural and Apostolical ; and we declare our firm and unanimous resolution, in dependence on Divine aid, to preserve those doctrines and that form of government, and to transmit them to our posterity." (Declaration of the Provincial Synod.)

That " it is not lawful for any man to take on him the office of public preaching, or ministering the sacraments in the congregation, before he be lawfully called, and sent to execute the same. And those we ought to judge lawfully called and sent, which be chosen and called to this work by men who have public authority given unto them in the congregation, to call and send ministers into the Lord's vineyard." (Art. xxiii.)

"That the book of consecration of Archbishops and Bishops, and ordering of Priests and Deacons, lately set forth in the time of Edward VI., is free from superstition and ungodliness, and contains all things necessary to such consecration and ordering, and that all consecrated or ordered, according to such rites are rightly, orderly, and lawfully consecrated and ordered." (Art. xxiii.)

The Church of England prays for " all Bishops, Priests and Deacons," (Litany) for "all Bishops and Curates," (prayer for clergy) for "Bishops and Pastors of Thy flock," for "divers orders in Thy Church," (Ember Collects, and St. Peter's Day) "for the ministers and stewards of Thy mysteries," (Coll. 3 Ad.), for "faithful and true pastors," (Coll. St. Matthias) for God's servants called to the order, or 'office,' and ministration of Deacons," and that they "may be found worthy to be called unto the higher ministries," (ordering of Deacons) for " God's servants called to the office of Priesthood," and "office and ministry," (Ordering of Priests) for " Bishops and Pastors of Thy flock," for "our brother elected," for "Thy servant called to the work and ministry of a Bishop," (Consecration of Bishop.)

The Preface to "the Form and manner of making, ordaining and consecrating of Bishops, Priests and Deacons," states. "It is evident to all men diligently reading the Holy Scripture and ancient authors, that from the Apostles' time there have been these orders of ministers in Christ's Church: Bishops, Priests and Deacons. Which offices were evermore had in such reverend estimation, that no man might presume to execute any of them, except he were first called, tried, examined, and known to have such qualities as are requisite for the same; and also, by public prayer, with imposition of

F

hands, were approved and admitted thereunto by lawful authority. And, therefore, to the intent that these orders may
be continued, and reverently used and esteemed, in the
Church of England, no man shall be accounted or taken to
be a lawful Bishop, Priest, or Deacon, in the Church of England, or suffered to execute any of the said functions, except
he be called, tried, examined and admitted thereunto, according to the form hereafter following, or hath had formerly
Episcopal consecration or ordination."

In the ordaining and making of priests and deacons, the
"necessity of these two orders in the Church of Christ" is
declared, and the distinct assertion is made, "that God, by
his Divine Providence, has divers orders of ministry in this
church, and that by this ministry "God's name ought to be
glorified, and His kingdom enlarged." In the ordering of
deacons, "the bishop, laying his hands on the head of every
one of them," confers the commission to fulfil the office in the
words, "Take thou authority to execute the office of a deacon
in the Church of God committed unto thee : In the Name of
the Father, and of the Son, and of the Holy Ghost. Amen."
In the ordering of priests, "the bishop, with the priests
present. shall lay their hands severally upon the head of
every one that receiveth the order of the priesthood," the
bishop saying, "Receive the Holy Ghost for the office and
work of a priest in the Church of God, now committed unto
thee by the imposition of our hands. Whose sins thou dost
forgive, they are forgiven ; and whose sins thou dost retain,
they are retained. And be thou a faithful dispenser of the
Word of God, and of His holy sacraments, In the Name of
the Father, and of the Son, and of the Holy Ghost. Amen."
Then, the bishop shall deliver to every one of them kneeling,
the Bible into his !hand, saying : "Take thou authority to
preach the Word of God, and to Minister the Holy Sacraments in the congregation, where thou shalt be lawfully appointed thereunto."

In the form for the consecration of bishops,—"The archbishop and bishops present, shall lay their hands upon the

head of the elected bishop, the [archbishop] saying, "Receive the Holy Ghost for the office and work of a bishop in the Church of God, now committed unto thee by the imposition of our hands, In the Name of the Father, and of the Son, and of the Holy Ghost. Amen. And remember that thou stir up the Grace of God which is given thee by this imposition of our hands; for God hath not given us the spirit of fear, but of power, and love, and soberness."

THE PRESBYTERIAN CHURCH

teaches "that Christ hath appointed for the edification of his Church," "extraordinary officers, as apostles, evangelists, and prophets, which have ceased, and ordinary and perpetual officers as pastors, teachers and other church governors and deacons." (1). The pastor or elder is to preach, to visit and pray for the sick, both in public and private, to pray for and with his flock, to read the Scriptures, to catechise, to dispense other divine mysteries, to administer the sacraments, to bless the people from God, to take care of the poor, and to rule his flock. The duties of these officers may be distributed in any one congregation, where there are several ministers, according to the gifts of such ministers. (2). Elders (of the people) joined in the government of the church with the ministers, by the institution of Christ. (3). Deacons, perpetual and distinct officers in the church, to whose office it belongs not to preach the Word or administer the Sacraments, but to take special care in distributing to the necessities of the poor.

Ordination is "the act of the Presbytery." The "power of ordering the whole work of ordination is in the whole Presbytery," and "every minister of the Word is to be ordained by imposition of hands and prayer, with fasting by those preaching Presbyters to whom it doth belong." The act of ordination is performed "by at least three or four ministers of the Word," appointed by the Presbytery, and is given by the imposition of hands and the following outlined prayer: "Thankfully acknowledging the great mercy of God in sending Jesus Christ for the redemption of his people, and for his ascension to the right hand of God the Father, and thence pouring out his Spirit and giving gifts to men, apostles, evangelists, prophets pastors and teachers, for the gathering and building up of his Church, and for fitting and inclining this man to this great work (here let them impose hands on his head), to entreat him to fit him with his Holy Spirit, to give him (who, in his name, we thus set apart to this Holy Service), to fulfil the work of his ministry in all things, that he may both save himself and his people committed to his charge." (The Form of Church Government. Confession of Faith).

According to the "Rules and forms of procedure of the Presbyterian Church in Canada," ordination is given as follows: "The presiding minister then engages in prayer, during which, by the laying on of the hands of the Presbytery, the candidate is solemnly set apart to the office of the Holy Ministry. After which the presiding minister gives him the right hand of fellowship, saying unto him: "In the name of the Lord Jesus Christ, the only King and Head of the Church, and by authority of the Presbytery of——I invite you to take part of this ministry with us, induct you to the pastoral charge of this congregation and admit you to all the rights and privileges thereto pertaining." Ruling elders are elected to office by the communicants of the congregation and are ordained with prayer by the moderator, the right hand of fellowship being given after the act. Deacons are also elected by the communicants and the same rules and forms are observed in their ordination as in the case of elders."

THE METHODIST CHURCH.

In the Methodist Church, a minister is "constituted by the election of the Annual Conference, and ordained by the laying on of the hands of those duly appointed thereto." The duties of a minister are (1) to conduct all parts of Divine worship; (2) to administer baptism and the Lord's Supper; (3) to solemnize matrimony, and, in general, to perform all the work of Christian service. The ordination service is a revised edition of the Church of England service for the ordering of priests, and the Act of Ordination is as follows: —" When this prayer is ended, the General Superintendent, with two or more of the ministers present, shall lay their hands severally upon the head of every one that receiveth the order of ministers; the receivers humbly kneeling upon their knees, and the General Superintendent saying, 'The Lord pour upon thee the Holy Ghost for the office and work of a minister in the Church of God, now committed unto thee by the imposition of our hands. And be thou a faithful dispenser of the Word of God, and of His holy sacraments, in the name of the Father, and of the Son, and of the Holy Ghost, Amen.' Then the General Superintendent shall deliver to every one of them, kneeling, the Bible into his hands, saying, ' Take thou authority to preach the Word of God, and to administer the holy sacraments in the congregation.' "

In the Standards of the Methodist Church, there is no formal definition of the ministry, or any authoritative teaching of a distinctive character, even on the subject of the Methodist ministry. Ministers are recognised as "appointed by the Holy Spirit in the Church," the "dignity of the office " is referred to, and a promise of reverent obedience to "chief ministers, to whom is committed the charge and government over you," is demanded, but beyond these, and like incidental teaching, the Methodist Standards appear almost without dogmatic teaching on this all important subject.

ON GOD'S ETERNAL DECREE: PREDESTINATION AND ELECTION.

THE CHURCH OF ENGLAND

teaches " that predestination to life is the everlasting purpose of God, whereby (before the foundations of the world were laid) He hath constantly decreed by His counsel, secret to us, to deliver from curse and damnation those whom He hath chosen in Christ out of mankind, and to bring them by Christ to everlasting salvation as vessels made to honour," etc., etc. (Art. xvii.)

THE PRESBYTERIAN CHURCH

teaches (1) That God ordains whatsoever comes to pass. (2) That he does not ordain as the result of fore-knowledge, but of his own free-will alone. (3) That by the decree of God, for the manifestation of his glory, some men and angels are pre-destinated unto everlasting life, and others fore-ordained to everlasting death. (4) These men and angels, thus pre-destinated and fore-ordained, are particularly and unchange-ably designed, and their number is so certain and definite, that it cannot be either increased or diminished. (5) Pre-destinated mankind are so of God's free grace, without any foresight of faith, or good works, or perseverance. (6) As God hath appointed the elect unto glory, so hath he fore-ordained all the means thereunto. (7) The rest of mankind God was pleased, etc., to pass by, and to ordain them to dis-honour and wrath for their sin, to the praise of His glorious justice. (Confess. Faith, Art. iii.)

THE METHODIST CHURCH

Has no Article or dogmatic teaching on this subject, with the exception of Wesley's 52nd Sermon, which may be fairly regarded as representing Methodist doctrine. In this ser-mon he teaches: (1) God knows all believers, not that His knowledge makes them to be such, but that it enables Him to foresee how they will, in the exercise of their freedom, become such. (2) He wills that all such should be saved from sin. (3) To that end He justifies them. (4) Sanctifies them. (5) Takes them to glory.

The Church of England and the Methodist Church are in practical agreement, as the Article of the former is capable of being interpreted on the lines of Wesley's sermon. Nothing is said in Article xvii. (Church of England) as to the "moving cause" of Predestination; and as that moving cause was distinctly stated in the Lambeth Articles to have been "the sole will of God" (which Articles were designed to express the Calvinistic doctrines), Arminians not unnaturally claim that the present Article expresses their own views.

Then both Churches are one in a practical rejection of the doctrine of "the reprobation of the Non-Elect," which is clearly taught by the Presbyterian Church in the Westminster Confession.

In connection with a tremendous doctrine of this nature, one might fairly hope that, out of a Christian Conference, some solution of existing difficulties might arise. That there must be an Article on the subject seems a necessity, but it might be so framed as, on the one hand, to acknowledge the sovereignty of God, and on the other, to allow the exercise of the right of private judgment as to how God uses that sovereignty for His own glory and the good of His Church.

———

That there are minor points of difference between these three great systems is probable, but one can see none of vital importance passed over in the foregoing review. May God grant that, as points of agreement are more clearly recognised and their value realised, a spirit may be born which may lead us to approach our differences as the long-parted brothers of the one household of faith, anxious, at least, to do what is best for the glory of God; and willing, if He make the way clear, to resign the cherished names of our past Church history, and to strike out anew in this new country as a branch of The Holy Catholic Church, the harbinger and prophecy of a wider unity yet to come.

THE END.

www.ingramcontent.com/pod-product-compliance
Lightning Source LLC
Chambersburg PA
CBHW032246080426

42735CB00008B/1018